THE HISTORY OF BAHAWALPUR

THE

HISTORY OF BAHAWALPUR,

WITH NOTICES OF THE ADJACENT COUNTRIES OF

SINDH, AFGHANISTAN, MULTAN, AND THE WEST OF INDIA.

BY

SHAHAMET ALI

GYAN

Published by

Gyan Publishing House
5, Ansari Road
Daryaganj, New Delhi-110002
Phone: 011-47034999, 9811692060
E-mail: books@gyanbooks.com

Distribution Network
gyanbooks.com
India, USA, Canada, UK, Australia, France

ISBN: 978-81-212-7945-1 (PB)
First Published, 1848

2nd Impression 2023

Printed at: Gyan Press, Delhi.

THE HISTORY OF BAHAWALPUR
Author: SHAHAMET ALI

THE HISTORY OF BAHAWALPUR.

THE
HISTORY OF BAHAWALPUR,

WITH NOTICES OF THE ADJACENT COUNTRIES OF

SINDH, AFGHANISTAN, MULTAN, AND THE WEST OF INDIA.

BY

SHAHAMET ALI,

AUTHOR OF "THE SIKHS AND AFGHANS."

LONDON:
JAMES MADDEN, 8, LEADENHALL STREET.

M.DCCC.XLVIII.

PREFACE.

THE Work, of which the following is an abstract, is an abbreviation of the family annals of Nawab Bahawal Khan. It was abridged at Bahawalpur by Peer Ibrahim Khan, the British native agent there, at the request of Captain J. D. Cunningham, an officer of acknowledged merit, and of extensive literary acquirements and information, as well as of political experience, and who is now our political agent at Bhopal. On his appointment to the latter agency in 1846, I became aware that he had some valuable Oriental MSS. in his possession, and asked him to give me some work, in which I might employ my leisure hours usefully to myself and to the public. He most liberally and readily gave me two MSS.; viz. one, the present work, and the other a religious book, written by the famous Molwee Mohammed Ismael, relating to the prevailing abuses and proper reform of the Mohammedan doctrines in India. I am therefore greatly indebted to this officer for the use of these manuscripts; and my most sincere acknowledgments are due to him. The information given in the introductory chapter is the result of my personal inquiries and observations made in 1833, when I accompanied the mission of Sir Claude Martine Wade, who was deputed to Bahawalpur by the British Government to open the navigation of the Sutlej, and returned overland through Dereh Ghazi Khan, Multan, and the extensive Barh, or wilderness, lying between Multan and Pak-Patan, the whole course never having been before traversed by any British officer. I am also indebted for further information to Peer Ibrahim Khan, who has now, among others, become known to the English people by his valuable services in suppressing the disturbances which have lately broken out in that quarter. For the matter contained in the supplementary chapter, and that in the Appendix about Dereh Ghazi Khan, I am indebted to the notes of Major Mackison, now our commissioner for the Cis-Sutlej territory, who also accompanied our mission in 1833, and resided at Bahawalpur as agent on the part of the British Government, which gave him a superior opportunity of acquiring an intimate knowledge of the country and tribes in that quarter. For these notes I have to thank Sir Claude Wade, who, in the full anticipation of Mr. Mackison's concurrence, has given me leave to use them.

I am also obliged to Professor Wilson for his kindness in correcting the proof sheets during my absence from London, and beg him to accept my sincere thanks for the same.

It will be unjust in me to close this preface without alluding briefly to the undeniable proofs which the ruling family of Bahawalpur have incessantly given of their fidelity and good-will towards the British Government. The Bahawalpur chief has always been one of the most faithful allies of that Government in India. The hospitable conduct of the ancestor of the present chief towards the mission of the Hon. Mr. Elphinstone in 1809 to Cabul is well known, and recorded by that gentleman himself. The good offices of the present chief on the occasion of the opening of the navigation of the Sutlej were conspicuous, when compared with the opposition of other parties; and the beneficial results to which they have since frequently led; and his co-operation in opening the land-route between Delhi and the Bahawalpur territory has been similarly advantageous* in encouraging the transit of trade through a sandy desert. The assistance rendered by him to the army of the Indus during its passage in 1838-39, is equally notorious and

* A corps of the Bundelcund contingent, amounting to 2000 men, on its way to Sindh, crossed by this route in 1843.

creditable. Without Bahawal Khan's active co-operation, in collecting supplies, and furnishing carriage, both by land and water, the British army would have been exposed to great trouble and inconvenience in passing the Bahawalpur territory. He also persevered in the same course during the wars in Sindh and the Punjab; and his recent achievements in coming forward to check the designs of Moolraj are at present the subjects of general admiration. It is owing to these ties of faithful attachment, as well as to the political position of the Bahawalpur territory, of which yet very little seems to be known, that I have been induced to present this work to the English public. I sincerely hope that a perusal of the political memoir of such a faithful ally will have some interest, not only for those directly connected with India, but to English readers generally.

For myself, I beg that indulgence of the reader to the imperfection of style which a foreign writer may justly claim.

NOVEMBER, 1848.

INTRODUCTION.

At the present time, the territory of Bahawalpur is bounded on the east by the British possessions of Sirsa, and on the west by the river Indus; the river Garra forms its northern boundary, and Bikaner and Jeyselmeer are on its southern frontier. Its length, from Rana-Wuttro on the east to Subzul-Kot on the west, is calculated at 216 koss, or 324 English miles. Its breadth varies much: in some parts it is eighty, and in others from sixty to fifteen miles.

Since the conquest of Sindh by the British Government, the districts of Subzul-Kot and Bhoongara, of which Bahawalpur had been dispossessed by the Ameers of Sindh, have been restored, as a reward for the Nawab's fidelity. In 1844, the Khan ceded to the British Government a strip of land on the Sutlej, bordering on the Sirsa frontier.

In the vicinity of the river, from within thirty to six miles, the land is rich and productive, but degenerates into an arid beach as it approaches the sandy desert to the south. The desert is incapable of cultivation. It is the resort of the Gullas of camels and other cattle, who find plenty of forage. In good seasons, the land commonly produces crops of Bajra, Moth, and barley; but they have had none for want of rain for the last twelve years.

There are twenty-one forts and strongholds situated in the desert, each being garrisoned by a party of troops, to protect the merchants and travellers.

The river Garra serves as a rich source of irrigation to the inhabitants occupying its banks. There are twenty canals cut from it, for the purpose of irrigation; but water flows into them only in the months of April and May, when the river rises, probably from the melting of the snow in the mountains; and for the rest of the year, with the exception of the height of the rainy season, the weather remains dry. There is, however, no need of rain, as a sufficient periodical supply of water is obtained from the above sources.

The harvest, or Rabee crops, are sown from the middle of September to the middle of January, while they commence mowing them from April to the end of May. The Khareef, or autumn crops, are sown between June and July, and cut down between October and December.

The products of the Rabee are chiefly wheat, barley, and other grain, while those of the Khareef consist of rice, Jowar, Bajra, Muka, and Moth. Sugar and indigo are also produced abundantly, and are among the staple articles exported to foreign countries. A kind of rice called Belanga, produced in the Khanpur district, is also exported in large quantity to Sindh. Among fruits which flourish in this climate are pomegranates, apples, mulberry, peach, grapes, lemons, oranges, mangoes, and Aloocha. Herbage of every kind peculiar to such a region is also produced in abundance. Potatoes do not yet appear to have been introduced. The government share is taken in kind, while the grain is yet in the stock, and varies from one-third to one-fifth of the produce.

REVENUE.—The collections being made in kind, it is difficult to calculate their exact amount; but the whole income is estimated at fourteen lakhs in Bahawalpur currency; viz., land revenue eleven lakhs, and customs and fees three lakhs. The rupee is an anna and a half less than the Company's coin. The annual disbursements, including the payment of the army and establishments, as well as sundry other charges, amounts in the whole to nine lakhs of rupees. Hence the yearly saving is five lakhs, and the public treasury must therefore be full.

CLIMATE.—It is rather hot and disagreeable to Europeans, and other people from cold climates. But, however, the natives of the land do not suffer from it, although much complaint is heard on the part of foreigners. The hot season is intolerably oppressive. During the months of July, August, and September, when the canals overflow with water, owing to the rise of the river, the villagers who occupy their banks are much annoyed by musquitoes having very painful stings. The people also partly suffer at the same time from fever; but the latter disease becomes most prevalent when they have much rain, which, however, is but seldom. During the whole rainy season, they have only one or two partial showers, and a similar quantity in winter.

FORM OF GOVERNMENT.—It is absolute, and the

order of succession is hereditary. The present chief attends to the business of state personally, being now and then, however, relieved in matters of small importance by his ministers. No oppression is allowed to be exercised towards the Ryots. The princes have no interference in state affairs. When the current business is over, visitors are admitted. All respectable servants and officers are allowed to pay their respects. The appearance of the Durbar is very respectable, and marked with regularity. They sit on carpets, in regular lines, according to their respective grades. If any one of the Sayids, Mullahs, or respectable Daoodputra chiefs comes in, the chief and the courtiers immediately rise to receive him. In short, I have not seen a more orderly Durbar. Much attention is paid to a stranger. During the continuance of the Durbar, the chief very seldom talks to his functionaries without necessity.

The Durbar is held from eight to twelve o'clock in the morning, when the chief retires, as is customary in every native court, to the Kehloola, or siesta; but the Bahawalpur Khan employs this time generally in reading. In the afternoon Durbar, the Khan is attended only by his sons and Motmids, or confidentials, and very little business is transacted at the time.

If a complaint of outrage is ever received in the court against any of the public officers, he is immediately summoned to the presence. On finding that the case deserves a regular inquiry, it is made over for investigation and decision to the Kazee, or judge, in attendance. Should the plaintiff be dissatisfied with his decision, the case is next referred for settlement to the town Kazee, or sometimes it is decided by the chief himself.

Each large town has a Kazee, a Kotwal or magistrate, and a Chodhree; the latter chiefly for regulating the prices, etc., of the markets. All judicial and criminal cases are referred, in the first instance, to the local authorities. The Kazee is the superior officer, and, with his permission, cases of small importance are also made over to the Kotwal, and the Chodhree. To the former only those of a criminal nature, and to the latter such as are connected with the bazar. But if any of these officers is unable to make a satisfactory settlement, the Kazee then takes the matter into his own hands. Should any one disobey the Kazee's orders, he is subjected to proper punishment, according to the Shara, or Mohammedan law. If any one is dissatisfied with the decision of the local authority, he appeals against it to court, when the Durbar Kazee is desired to make proper inquiries. He collects some other Mullahs, and, along with them, enters into a reinvestigation of the matter, and reports the result, with his own opinion, to the chief, who generally acquiesces in his decision. There is no appeal against this decree.

Besides the perquisites enjoyed by the local Kazee on the part of the government, he levies a fee, or Mohrana, on deeds drawn out in his office, and sealed with his seal. The amount of fees is fixed at a rupee and a quarter per paper, without reference to its importance. It is levied from the owner of the paper. A periodical register of this income is prepared and sent regularly to court, for the information of the chief.

There is a news-writer also attached to each large

town. His business is to transmit to court a report of all passing occurrences. There is a Nakara, or kettle-drum, assigned to each Kotwalee, with a drummer, whose duty it is to beat the Nakara thrice every night, from sunset till about eleven o'clock. At the last beating, all passing to and fro is stopped. If a stranger is, however, found moving about after that hour, he is seized and kept in custody by the watchmen until morning, when he is again set at liberty.

Notwithstanding the many precautions on the part of the chief, his functionaries are very corrupt, and very oppressive towards the Ryots. If any instance of this nature is brought before him, he inflicts proper punishment on the guilty. Yet they do not improve in their conduct, but take care that, if possible, no such complaint shall reach his ears. Hence the ruler is very popular, and loved by his people, while his functionaries are comparatively hated. Complaints against them are loud and general.

Although the country is known by the name of the Daoodputras, yet there are very few of that tribe in comparison with other inhabitants. The Daoodputras of the middle class, who attend the summons of the chief when necessary, are about seven or eight thousand men. They are thus divided:—

Shuter Sawars, or camel-riders . .	2,000
Horsemen	2,900
Footmen	4,000
	8,000

To each man is allotted fifty Beegahs of land. These Jaghirdars are termed Jaghirdar-Lushker. The Daood-putras trace their origin to Abbas, the uncle of Mohammed the prophet, as is apparent from the history. They are divided into four principal branches; viz. Peerjanee, to which the reigning family belongs, as well as Kehranee, Arbanee, and Khemranee. These branches are subdivided into several other offshoots.

ARMY.—The number above stated is a kind of militia of the country. They are bound to wait on the chief in time of emergency, when their attendance is required. Besides, the state maintains a standing army, consisting of about seven thousand men in all, exclusive of the police and district *Sebandies*.

Captain, now Major Mackison, while at Bahawalpur, has given the following account of the Nawab's forces. "The other forces (besides the feudatories maintained by the Khan), consist of:—1st, Five regiments of regular infantry, the whole of which together do not muster more than twelve or thirteen hundred men. They are a miserable rabble, without a shadow of discipline, and consist chiefly of Parbeeas, runaway sipahis from the eastward. 2nd, Twelve hundred Bargir horsemen; the horses and arms are the property of the Sirkar. The men receive two rupees' worth of rations, and six rupees pay per month. They are chiefly kept in attendance on the Khan and his principal officers. 3d, Five hundred foreign and Musaffir Sawars. The men furnish their own arms and horses, and receive from ten to twelve rupees as pay. The forts in the desert are garrisoned by foot-soldiers, chiefly of the Moher caste. Their number is stated at two thousand two hundred men. The artillery consists of sixteen guns, for eight of which the establishment of Golundas and bullocks is kept up. There are, it is said, upwards of forty guns, including those in the forts, but few are in a serviceable state.

The Jaghirdars, when employed on a distant duty, take their retainers on camels, as was the case when I visited the country in 1833, and subsequently in 1840.

POPULATION.—It consists of almost all general tribes of Hindu and Mussulmans; but the latter predominate. Among the Hindus there are many of the Kara tribe. The Daoodputras about the court, and the merchants, are the only principal people, and in affluent circumstances; while the rest of the population appear to be in a sad state of destitution. The villagers are rather dirty, as is perhaps the case throughout India; but the Sindhees and Bahawalpurs are proverbial in this point. The latter are very shy and timid. If they see a Feringee, or any of his people passing by the way, they conceal themselves, for fear of being seized in Begar. They are, however, courteous in manners among themselves.

MANNERS AND CUSTOMS.—The intercourse among the people of the first class is very limited. They seldom visit each other without necessity. A foreigner is, however, treated with attention; yet he is never considered equal in point of rank or honour. A Daoodputra is very fond of his home, and seldom leaves it in search of employment for a foreign country. The Sayids and Mullahs are not ashamed of begging about. Although many blasphemies prevail among them, yet they consider themselves very religious characters. The Mullahs are chiefly of the Soofee sect. They have no objection to listen to singing, especially of moral songs. The custom of making proselytes is very prevalent; nay, it is considered a kind of trade by them, because they generally live on the bounty of their followers. The making of Tazia, and reciting Mirsia, or mournful poems in memory of Hassan and Hussain, in the month of Mohurrum, is entirely prohibited by Government, and is considered an unpardonable transgression. Polygamy is very prevalent. Marrying one, two, and three women, is supposed an honourable act, with a view to propagate offspring. Even those of the poorest classes have not less than two wives, though they have hardly means to support them. It is customary among common people, that if any one may not like his wife, he goes straight to the Kazee, and obtains a deed of divorce, on the payment of the stipulated Mahr.* The amount of the Mahr in this country does not, among the lower classes, exceed twenty-five rupees. Besides, the husband pays to the woman an additional sum for her support for four months, at the rate of three quarters of a seer of atta, and a couple of pice per diem. The interval between the divorce and re-marriage is called Iddat. Iddat is the period a woman counts after being divorced. It is not more than four months and ten days. Before the

* Mahr is a sum stipulated on occasion of the marriage, to be paid to the wife by the husband, which is a debt that must be paid, unless voluntarily remitted by the former.

time of the prophet it was a complete year. After this, the woman is at liberty to marry any per on she likes. Should a wife be disgusted with her husband, she is also at liberty to obtain her separation, on remitting her claim to the stipulated Mahr, and she may marry another person if she chooses.

As soon as a man obtains his majority, the first thing he thinks of is to marry; but the people generally intermarry in their own tribe. Yet, however, if the marriage takes place, for instance between an Afghan and a woman of low caste, their issue is not considered in any degree degraded. Such child can be married without objection to a girl of pure blood, as well as the issue of parents of equal caste.

People in prosperous circumstances make much rejoicing on the approach of a marriage. Nakaras, or kettle-drums, are beaten on the occasion, and friends of both sexes entertained at night. The hired bands of dancers form themselves in a circle, and begin to dance as the Nakaras are beaten. Their movements are, however, not graceful or pleasing; but they are, at the same time, very amusing to the native spectators. This amusement is called Johneir-Bazee. It is followed by dances of the dancing girls, which last two or three days. On the last day, a general entertainment is given to the whole tribe. The same night, the marriage party proceeds in procession to the dwelling of the bride; and, after the marriage ceremony is performed, the latter is transferred in a Dola, a kind of litter, to the house of the husband, followed by the party.

The father of the girl gives her on the occasion as

many ornaments and other things in dowry as his means and liberality will admit. Among other things, she is especially presented with a pair of bangles, made of ivory. This custom also prevails among all Rajpoots.

If, on such occasions, one is not disposed to give grand parties, accompanied with dancings, he is accused by the people of his tribe of parsimony, and the party is styled that of mourning. I am sorry to add, that such notions prevail throughout India. People, even though in debt, try to give grand parties, though otherwise they may be actually starving. What is more wonderful is, that though almost every one acknowledges the absurdity of such foolish ceremonies, yet they are obliged to follow the custom, to save their reputation. I wish the Indians, miserable and wretched as they have lately become in their pecuniary and political position, would learn to be wise.

FOOD.—The food of the people generally consists of unleavened bread, with the flesh of sheep or goats. They are exceedingly fond of fish; but the common people prefer beef, which is cheaper. The eating of Dawl, which is so common in other parts of Hindustan, is looked upon with contempt. If any one, from poverty, is obliged to use it, he is despised by his neighbours as a miser; and, as such, becomes the subject of scandal. The Mussulmans and Hindus, who can afford it, also indulge in drinking. The latter, moreover, have no objection to eat mutton and game, such as partridges and Taderoe, the famous Cypress bird, fabled to be in love with fire. They also eat fish. The lower classes chiefly use Bhang, the well-known intoxicating drug in India.

In-door Amusements.—Besides the amusement of cards, chess, etc., some of them indulge in dancing parties, and other idle amusements; and others, though in a very limited degree, in reading books.

Out-door Amusements.—Field sports form the chief out-door amusement of men of the first, and of the middle classes especially; for a shooting excursion is the favourite amusement of the Daoodputras. In the afternoon, the people generally go out to amuse themselves in gardens (of which there are many, after the fashion of the Punjab), and sit on the banks of the canals, etc., till sunset, when they return home. In the summer, their amusements are on a higher scale. From May to August, they pass the day in gardens, and there give parties to friends, who are amused at the same time with the dances and similar treats. Sundays are chiefly past on the banks of brooks and running waters. In short, for four months they employ themselves in similar entertainments. These parties terminate by bathing in a river, if practicable, on the last Sunday, which act is considered among the most propitious.

On Joma, or Friday, the Mussulmans assemble in the Jameh-masjid, to hear the preaching of Mullahs, and also resort to other religious assemblies of the Soofee sect. They are fond of going out to fairs too, whenever they take place.

Dress.—The dress partakes of the Sindh and the Punjab fashion. There is very little difference between the dress of a Hindu and a Mussulman; so it is difficult for a stranger to know, merely from external appearances, to which class a person belongs. Men of high class generally use a Lungee, or scarf, with embroidered borders, which they throw across their shoulders downward, as well as a large turban, and an Angarkha, or long coat, with broad trousers, fitting tight in the end. In winter they also use a Chogha, or cloak ; and instead of a cotton turban, use a shawl. Those who attend the Durbar generally use a neat dress, consisting of silk, etc. Under the turban they always have a Kolah or cap, sometimes a cotton scull-cap. The religious people generally have a cap called Kolaha-kadree, and a long waistcoat or Kurta, with trousers. Being in the habit of using snuff, they carry about them a pocket handkerchief. They are not addicted to smoking.

The dress of the people in general is not clean. They wear their beards, and allow their hair to grow in long locks down their shoulders. To keep the hair well oiled is considered beneficial to the head: hence, their dress about the shoulders is generally stained with grease.

Lungees and silk goods, manufactured at Bahawalpur. are much used. English chintz and other cloth, are also in common use, but not universally. They are not in the habit of using ornaments and jewels, as is the custom of their neighbours, the Sikhs.

The dress of women consists of broad trousers, and a small waistcoat, and a Lungee, which makes the exterior covering. They are fond of using the silk produced in their own country. Their ornaments are generally made of gold and silver, and they prefer enamelled work.

Ivory bangles are commonly used by a woman of high class, especially if a bride.

These women, like other Mohammedan ladies, remain in seclusion. The Hindu women, imitating the custom of their neighbours, are also of retired habits.

EDUCATION.—The common people are mostly illiterate and much in darkness. Some of the higher class, however, give a limited education to their children in the Persian and Arabic languages. The Rora people are for the most part (though only partially) conversant with reading and writing. They serve as writers under the Daoodputras, or hangers-on about the court. The Bummons and Khatrees receive instruction in Sanscrit, but on a very limited scale.

Their own mother language is a mixture of Sindhee and the Punjabee. A person understanding either of the two tongues will find very little difficulty in understanding a Daoodputra.

PROFESSIONAL PURSUITS.—The greater portion of the population is agricultural: very few are in service. Many are employed in manufacturing goods of various kinds. Both silk and cotton cloths are produced in Bahawalpur; cotton and woollen carpets of the best kind are also manufactured. The weavers are remarkable for their ingenuity and quick understanding; they can imitate any cloth of any country. Gold-thread is prepared abundantly; earthen pots, such as water-jugs, etc. are very delicately made. There is also a good watch-maker, named Azim-ud-Deen, in the employ of the Nawab,

Some persons can write a very good Persian and Arabic hand.

Trade.—Since the opening of the navigation of the Sutlej and Indus, in 1833, and also the opening of the land route from Delhi to Bahawalpur, across the desert, by way of Sersa, much merchandise is in transit through this territory. On the Delhi road several wells, at intervals of two koss, and caravanseries, at every stage are said to have been built for the accommodation of travellers and merchants. Chokees of Sipahis have also been stationed at proper distances, to protect the line, so that a merchant can travel with greater safety than before; a moderate scale of duty having been at the same time levied to ensure traffic by this route. This road was opened during the administration of Lord Ellenborough, who in 1845 deputed Mr. Hamilton, now the political resident at Indore, for that purpose. It is the thoroughfare of the trade going on between the countries beyond the Indus and India.

Exports.—The exports chiefly are made to Rajpootana in the east; and Sindh, Bombay, and Afghanistan to the south-west. They consist of wheat, rice, indigo, sugar, and silk.

Imports.—English fine and coarse cloth; Kerana or spices from the Punjab; and fruits and horses from Afghanistan.

The inland trade is chiefly carried on by land, except in the vicinity of the Garra, where goods are principally conveyed by water. Camels are the principal means of conveyance. The trade is mostly confined to the Hindus.

Bahawalpur, the capital, is the mart of the Bahawalpur territory. It is situated about two miles on the left bank of the river Garra. Besides this place, there are other commercial towns also of note, such as Ahmedpur, Khanpur, Uch, etc., and others of smaller note.

In addition to the little sketch I have given of Bahawalpur, I think it as well to subjoin notes and observations of the same nature regarding the adjoining and equally important province of Multan, which is of particular interest at the present moment.

In the reign of the Emperor Akbar, the province of Multan consisted of eighty-two Mahals. At that time it was one of the largest provinces in the empire, and comprehended, besides Multan proper, the adjoining countries of Beloochistan, Sindh, Shwestan, Tatta, and Bhakr. When the institutes of Akbar were composed towards the end of that monarch's reign, the limits formerly possessed by the provinces were greatly diminished. Since the dominion of the Sihks, its former divisions have, like those of Lahore, experienced considerable changes. Its present boundaries are the Sutlej to the east; on the west, the course of the Indus; to the north, the southern confines of the province of Lahore, and on the south the territory of Bahawalpur, extending to Uch and Mithankot, to which, in 1836, the Sikhs added the Mazaree territory; of which province it is not easy to define the actual extent; but its length may be estimated from Kot Kamalia to Mithankot, and its breadth from the western frontiers of Bahawalpur to Keroor on the Indus. The northern parts of the province are fertile, being watered by the Chenab, Jhelem, and Ravee. The part which lies between the Chenab and the Indus is, to the west, above Multan, chiefly a sandy desert. To the south, below that city, is generally a marsh of reeds and grass; and the country which intervenes between Multan and Bahawalpur is close, woody, and scantily peopled.

The city of Multan is supposed to be one of great antiquity, and to have been known at different times by various names, Hestpur, Bhakarpur, etc.; and among Europeans it is thought to be the site of the Malli of Alexander. It stands about three koss from the Chenab, is about three koss in circumference, built entirely of bricks, and surrounded by a wall of the same material, with six gates. The streets are close and irregular. About fifty paces to the east of the city there is a very old citadel, consisting of forty towers and four gates. The walls of it are extremely high, measuring nearly fifty feet, and originally it had no ditch, but since it fell into the power of the Sikhs, a ditch faced with masonry has been added to it by direction of Maharajah Runjeet Sing, besides two outworks, one before the Lukhee and the other before the Lahoree gates. The circumference of the citadel is about seventeen hundred paces. Inside the citadel there is a bazar. Both it and the city were formerly very populous. Since its capture by the Sikhs, and the defeat and dispersion of the Afghans, who were attached to the late government of Nawab Muzuffir Khan, it has lost its former wealth and prosperity. Many parts of the city are now completely deserted; and the Sikhs have scarcely left a trace of the range of buildings which constituted the residence of the Nawab and his officers, having taken the bricks to construct the ditch formed by them round the citadel. Outside there are several fine tombs, and two inside the citadel, which claim particular attention; one, the tomb of a Mohammedon saint, named Sheikh Baha-ud-Deen, Zikeria, and the other of his grandson Rookon-ud-Deen-i-Alum. They are both highly ornamented with Mosaic work. Within the citadel near the Deo gate there is a Hindu temple which the people call *Nursingh-ootar.* It is built of stone and contains twenty-five pillars. According to the legends of the Hindus, there was a great tyrant in that part of the country who wished to be considered a god. In one of his visits to the temple, a tiger came forth from one of the pillars and relieved the world of the tyrant and his oppressions by killing him, immediately after which the tiger disappeared. There are numerous Musjids within the city. That founded by Allee Mohammed Khan, the grandfather of Muzuffir Khan, is the most remarkable. The environs of the city are composed of a variety of gardens and orchards. They amount altogether to seventy. There are many of them, however, which are neglected and going to decay. Two of them, made by Nawab Muzuffir Khan, are described as being well worthy of observation. Close to the walls of the city there are also the remains of several Gurhees, or fortified houses, in which the Afghans of rank used to dwell.

The site of the city, as well as of the citadel, is a rising ground. Formerly the Chenab flowed below its walls. The land now lying between it and the river is a low cultivated track. Men of all trades and professions are settled here. It is famous for its brocaded silks, the strength and colour of which are greatly admired. They generally consist of large scarfs and striped pieces for Piejamahs or trousers, and are in great demand among the natives of the Punjab. There is besides a kind of chintz fabricated at Multan, stamped with gold and silver flowers, which is also held in great estimation. Its carpets, or Satrinjees, are also celebrated, but are very inferior to those of Persia.

From the low and marshy nature of the country south of Multan, there are few towns or villages in that direction of any distinction, excepting Shujahabad and Kot-i-Shuja, which are more military posts than towns. Northward, thirty koss from Multan and three from the left bank of the Ravee, stands the tower of Tiloomba, formerly a very populous place. It has now few inhabitants. A few paces to the south of the town is a square fort of masonry, with towers at each angle. It was built as a defence against the incursions of the wild tribes who occupy the Gunjee Barh, a woody track which commences within five koss south of the fort. The Zemindars of Tiloomba are of the Kathia tribe. They are settled in the Barh, and infest the country by their depredations as far as Multan. The Gunjee Barh extends with some open intervals from Sheikhoopoora and Lahore to the confluence of the united streams of the Jhalam, Chinab and Ravee, with the Sutlej at Uch. For some distance above and below Multan towards the Indus is an arid sandy track.

Across the Ravee, twenty-five koss from Tiloomba, towards Lahore, occurs the town of Herapah. The Ravee flows east of it. The Zemindars here are also Kathias, and addicted to plunder. Twenty-five koss to the north-west of Herapah, near a place called Sadoollapur, is a complete waste, which it is difficult to pass without joining a Kafilah, in consequence of the predatory habits of the neighbouring people and the scarcity of water. The density of the trees about Herapah is so great as to present no opening to the sight. It is quite a thicket.

Although twenty-five koss distant from each other, Tiloomba and Herapah are always called collectively by the same name. In speaking of the two people, either is named indiscriminately, there being no intermediate town or place of note.

Eastward of Multan, about eleven koss from the Sutlej, stands Depalpur. It is an ancient city interspersed with ruins. Among them is a fort, the walls of which appear to have been very high and strong. They exhibit traces of more than eighty large towers, each containing a well. It was formerly the seat of a separate provincial authority of great importance, and occurs often in the history of these countries. The inhabitants of the place, and generally of the country in its vicinity, are Daghars, Wetoohs, and Goojers, of a hardy and independent character, always noted for their turbulent impatience of authority. They are addicted to a life of depredation, though they possess large herds of cattle. During the rains, the Sutlej and Biah overflow their banks and inundate the whole of the intervening land. After they subside, it becomes a marshy wilderness, covered with reeds and bushes.

Opposite Depalpur, the river divides into several channels, which insulate the country and afford the tribes who inhabit these alluvial islands great security from the attacks of their neighbours. The Maharajah exacts an annual contribution from them, chiefly in bullocks for his artillery, and *ghee* or clarified butter for feeding his horses.

About thirteen koss to the south-east of Depalpur is the town of Putten, called Pak-Putten from containing the tomb of a distinguished saint named Sheikh Fareed-ud-Deen Shakerganj. A pilgrimage to it is considered meritorious among the superstitious Mohammedans and Hindus; and every year, on the 5th of the month of Mohurrum, a large fair is held there, to which many people resort. The descendants of the saint were the hereditary proprietors of the place, as well as several dependent villages. The chief had the title of Dewan. Runjeet Sing deprived them of their possessions; and they now live by the alms and contributions of their disciples and the numerous pilgrims who frequent the shrine of their ancestors.

Near the termination of the Doab of Retchna, within five koss of the Chenab is the town of Jelalpur Kamlana. It is the chief place of a small district, which comprehends fifteen villages, peopled by the tribe of Kamlana. In the time of Muzuffir Khan it contained many inhabitants, but it is now depopulated, owing to the violence and rapacity of the Sikhs, being on the high road from Lahore to Multan, and thereby constantly exposed to the vexatious exactions of the Sikh soldiery.

Shirkot, about seven koss north-east of Jelalpur, was also another place of importance in Muzuffir Khan's time, but is now reduced to insignificance from the same cause which occasioned the desertion of Jelalpur. A little westward of the town is an extremely high mound, which once formed the site of the town. The Barh of Sundel commences from Shirkot, and the country immediately around it is thickly set with trees. There is a post established here for collecting duties on the transit trade between Multan and Lahore.

About fifteen koss to the east of Shirkot is Kotkamalia. There are many villages attached to it. The lands belong to the tribe of Khurl. In the east quarter of the city is a fort built of bricks. The people here are chiefly engaged in rearing camels. Twenty koss from it, on the road to Multan, Runjeet Sing constructed a large well with a flight of steps to lead down to the water; and also a compact little mud fort to keep the predatory inhabitants in that neighbourhood in order. Travellers could not pass it before without the chance of being plundered or murdered.

Three koss below the junction of the Chenab and Ravee, in the Doab of Baree, is Sirdarpur, a large town. The river flows by it. It possesses a strong fort, and has many dependent villages. The proprietors are all Pathans. At the point where the two rivers meet is a very considerable ferry called Fazilshah, by which the communication with that part of the Punjab and the countries on the Indus is principally maintained. In the vicinity of the ferry between the two rivers, there is a place belonging to a Fakeer, near which stands a very large Banian or Barh tree, famous for its great age and possessing immensely large trunks from one root, from which circumstance it is well known in that part of the country by the name of Ath-moodhee, or Eight Props.

Thirteen koss west from Munkeir is a large town called Kersar. The land about it is rich and flourishing. It is two and a half koss from the left bank of the Indus, and four from the skirts of the desert in which Munkeir stands, and seventeen koss north of Dereh Ismael Khan. In the immediate vicinity of the place is the tomb of a holy man, named Sheikh Lal Hussein, who was a distinguished disciple of Sheikh Bahawal Huj of Multan, and whose descendants are the sole proprietors of the lands attached to the town.

Inland, south-east of the Dereh Ismael Khan, is the town of Bhakar, a considerable place, with a mud fort consisting of twelve towers, but no ditch. It is considered of importance from its situation in that part of the frontier, and is occupied by a garrison of Runjeet Sing's troops.

Rangpur Kharis is another town of note in the province. It stands within five koss of the right bank of the Jhalem, and nineteen koss due north of the city of Multan. It has declined considerably in population from what it was when the Afghans were in possession of the province. Detached from the town is a fort.

Following the course of the Jhalem, twenty-two koss above Rangpur, is another considerable place, called Gher Maharaja, fortified by a mud-wall. The river passes within two koss of it, and there is a large ferry opposite.

HISTORY OF BAHAWALPUR,

AND OF

SOME OF THE ADJACENT PLACES.

In the reign of the Calif Abdul-Malek, the son of Merwan, agents were deputed by that sovereign to Sindh, to purchase a few slave-girls, and other rarities of the country. Having executed their commission, the agents returned by sea; and, on touching at the Loharee port, connected with Sindh, they were attacked by a party of pirates, when some were killed, and others fell into the hands of the pirates, with their precious charge. The few who escaped reported the occurrence to the Calif on their return to the capital. The Calif was highly incensed at the failure and sufferings of the deputation, and resolved on punishing the audacity of the pirates at the earliest opportunity. He did not, however, survive to carry out his resolve; but his son Walid, on his accession, directed Hajaj, who was employed in quelling a revolt in Kirman, to prepare an expedition to Sindh, to demand restitution. A large army was accordingly assembled for the purpose, and the command was given to his own cousin and son-in-law, Mohammed Casim, by whom, in the year 92 Hijra (710, A.D.), it was conducted to Mekran, which he made his place of rendezvous. Thence he immediately proceeded to commence his hostile operations against Sindh. Rao Dahir, the chief of Sewistan, was fully prepared to meet him; but he was dissuaded from his purpose by his advisers, who suggested to him to act for the present on the defensive. The Mussulmans consequently passed on to Neron Koh (now Hyderabad), and occupied that fortification without any opposition. The occupation of Neron led also to the taking of Tatta, which soon after fell into the hands of the invaders. Some of the "true believers" who were found prisoners in the fort, were immediately set at liberty, and sent back to the capital. Flushed with victory, Casim advanced upon Sewistan and Ahir; but here he was met by Rao Dahir, at the head of a considerable force; and a very bloody battle ensued between the two armies. At first, the enemy gained some decided advantage; but, ultimately, were totally routed, and obliged to take shelter in the fort of Abhor.

While Casim was meditating on the plan of reducing the place, he was joined by a Brahmin who had deserted his former master, the Rao. This man was immediately taken into favour, and soon raised to high rank. Owing to his great abilities and merits, he quickly gained the confidence of his new master. The settlement of the newly acquired territory, as well as the introduction of Mohammedan rule in Sewistan, was left entirely to his management. Casim himself, having recovered from the fatigues of the late bloody action, advanced to the neighbourhood of Abhor. He was again opposed by Dahir at the head of 10,000 horse and 30,000 foot, with many elephants. In ten days they had seven indecisive combats, in which the Mussulmans were however always successful. On the 10th Ramzan, 93 Hijra (711, B.C.), the Rao made a desperate attack; but in the heat of the action, his elephant was struck with a fire-ball, which so frightened the animal as to make him suddenly quit the field with his master, who was also mortally wounded with an arrow. The Rao's sudden disappearance spread confusion and terror in his army, which yielded and left his enemies masters of the field. The following day Casim made his triumphant entry into the fort of Abhor, and took possession of the whole property and treasure belonging to the fallen chief. The inferior treasures and a number of prisoners were sent off to Damascus to the Calif. Among the latter were the two daughters of the Rao Dahir.

A general amnesty was now announced to all the petty chieftains, and they were called on to tender unconditional allegiance to the new government.

The heads of the Cheena tribes were among the first who waited on the conqueror to evince their attachment, by presenting him with the best of their productions. They were received and treated in a conciliatory manner, and were still further gratified by the conduct of Casim in reducing their land-revenue to a tithe, in addition to allowing them an unaltered rate of custom-dues, without any demand on the part of the new government. Hence the people of the Cheena tribe who occupy the land along the right bank of the Indus are called "Ashree" or subject to the payment of a tithe.

The protection of government was also promised and extended to the tribes inhabiting the lands about Sabree, while they on their part were bound to maintain the safety of the road between Arabia and Sindh.

On the discomfiture of Rao Dahir, his sons shut themselves up in the fort of Askanda. As long as they continued in arms, Casim did not consider the safety of his territory secured; and he in consequence proceeded against them with such a force, that, notwithstanding their gallant and desperate defence, they could not hold out long, and the Mussulmans carried the place by a vigorous storm, in which the young men were slain, thus leaving the ambitious victor to the full enjoyment of his conquest, without further opposition or disturbance.

The conquest of Sindh having been thoroughly completed, Casim advanced upon Multan, which seems to have fallen without any opposition. His unresisted success encouraged him to achieve additional conquests; and with this view he organised an army on a larger scale. About 50,000 Mohammedans are said to have collected around his standard on this occasion. At the head of this army he penetrated into Hindustan by the way of Depalpur, and proceeded as far as Kunoj, without meeting any serious opposition in his progress. After establishing the Mohammedan rule by garrisoning every large town, the victorious army retraced its steps westward.

While Casim was engaged in aggrandizing the Mohammedan dominions by his bold exploits in Hindustan, he was visited by a sudden misfortune at home. We have already seen that among other presents, which he had sent to the Calif on the fall of Abhor, were the two daughters of Rao Dahir. On their arrival at Damascus, owing to their attractive beauty, they were readily admitted into the harem of the Calif. When one of them was brought into his presence, in order to retaliate and revenge the death of her father, she falsely stated that she was unworthy the honor of his bed, as her chastity had been forcibly taken from her by Casim, on the day of their capture. The Calif was highly incensed at the insult of his officer, and at the first impulse of his passion issued a vindictive mandate, peremptorily directing Casim to be sewn alive in a hide. When this unwarrantable order arrived, he was in the neighbourhood of Udaypur, and like a loyal servant, submitted to the sentence of his unjust master without the least hesitation or murmur.

For two years after this occurrence, the Hindus seem to have continued quiet under the Mohammedan rule; but they afterwards threw off the yoke which was forcibly imposed upon them, and succeeded in recovering their territory from the hands of the foreigners. The tract of country between the sea and Depalpur, however, still continued in the hands of Mussulmans.

In the year 132 Hijra (749, A.D.), a revolution broke out in the government of the Calif, which led to the expulsion of the Ommeid dynasty, and the succession of the house of Abbas. The first of that dynasty who ascended the throne was Abul-Abbas.

Governors were sent out by the new government to Sindh and the Punjab, of which they took possession without much resistance. The Abbas house continued in the enjoyment of their Indian possessions without molestation, until the Califat of Kader-Billah, being a period of 286 lunar years. After this period, peace was again disturbed by the hostile advance of Sultan Mahmood of Ghaznee, who, at the head of a large army overran the intermediate country between Ghaznee and Multan. Thence he pursued his successful career towards Sindh, and occupied the whole country in a short time. The Arabians who had settled in the country for several generations were treated kindly, and suitable pensions were assigned for their future support; but they were not allowed to have a voice in the politics of the country. As soon as the country had again subsided into quiet, Mahmood returned to Khorasan.

Up to Hijra 445 (1053, A. D.), Sindh was retained in the hands of the Ghaznee monarchs; but in the reign of Abdurrashed, the grandson of Mahmood, it was taken from them through the indolence of the prince. The Arabian colony nevertheless still continued in the country.

About this time, the Turks had attained great ascendancy in Kharizm and Khorasan; and not contented with their present possessions, aspired to aggrandise their dominions by annexing the neighbouring countries. Mangoo Khan, the grandson of Changiz Khan, detached a large army under the command of Halaku Khan, his brother, to extend his supremacy from the Oxus to Asia Minor and Syria, and also to demand the allegiance of the Bagdad Calif. Halaku Khan, after establishing the Turkish authority in the intermediate country, advanced upon Bagdad, of which Mossim Billah was at that time Calif. Prolonged overtures for negociation appear to have at first taken place between the two parties; but as the terms were considered derogatory to the high dignity of the Abbas house, the matter ended in a well-contested battle under the walls of Bagdad. The Turks eventually gained the day; and the Calif, with a company of Mullahs and Saids, threw himself upon the mercy of the victorious Halaku Khan.

The brutality, however, of this man was not satisfied by the humility of his fallen opponent; and having raised himself to the throne of Bagdad, 9th Safer, Hijra 656 (1258, A. D.), he savagely directed the conquered Calif to be sewed up in a felt, and to be pressed to death in a Shikonja, or rack. The sons, and other members of the family, also fell victims to the sword of this remorseless enemy. According to Muntakhab-ul-tawarikh, a general massacre was ordered, and 600,000 innocent lives are said to have been destroyed.

The above authority also states, that there were fifty-two Califs of the house of Abbas, that thirty-seven of them ruled over Bagdad, and that the period of their combined reign extended to a somewhat less period than 524 years. The other branch consisted of fifteen individuals; one of them was Sultan Ahmed, the son of Sultan Tahir, who, on the downfall of the Abbaside dynasty at Bagdad, emigrated to Egypt, where he was received by the government with open arms, and at once proclaimed the ruler of the country in Hijra 659 (1260, A. D.)

The Abbas house reigned here for two centuries; but in 919 (1551, A. D.), their power was again destroyed by the invasion of Salim Shah, one of the adventurous rulers of Constantinople. Mowakul Ali, the last Calif, was taken prisoner; and with him the Abbas house ended in Egypt.

According to the Muntakhab-ul-tawarikh, the two branches thus ruled over Bagdad and Egypt for 784 years.

INVASION OF SINDH BY AHMED VI.

For five generations, the succession was maintained in Egypt in the direct line, commencing with Sultan Ahmed; but the last sultan, Ahmed, having first given up the throne in favour of his heir, set out on an expedition to Sindh at the head of a body of 12,000 horse, chiefly consisting of the Abbas race. He made Mekran the point of invasion. Rao Dhorang, of the Fatteh tribe, who then ruled the country, marched to oppose the approaching enemy; but was terrified by a horrible dream, which caused him to purchase peace at the sacrifice of a third of his territory, which was voluntarily made over to Sultan Ahmed. He, moreover, conciliated him by giving him his daughter in marriage. A fortified town was likewise built after his own name; the ruins of which are to be seen to this day.

From this time, the historians seem to distinguish Ahmed by the title of Ameer. He had three sons by his Hindu wife: the eldest of whom was named Abu Nasir, otherwise Ameer Ibn, who succeeded his father on his death in his newly acquired principality. Rao Dhorang was succeeded by his son Jhokur. A serious misunderstanding took place soon after between the two young princes, and they appear to have immediately resorted to arms; but the young Rao, feeling his inability to cope with his antagonist with any degree of success in the field, retired to the fort of Tatta. The

Ameer demanded, as a condition of peace, that he should give him the hand of his daughter. The offer was rejected with scorn; and this led to a severe assault on Tatta, without, however, any decisive success. These operations at length terminated in a peace, through the advice of a mutual friend, when a matrimonial alliance was also arranged between the Ameer Ibn, and the daughter of Rao Jhokur, by whom he had a son he named Abd-ul Kahir, well known as Kahir Khan, who succeeded at his father's death. As soon as the new king was seated on the throne, he prepared an expedition against Parkher, which he reduced by a protracted siege. The governor of the place, who was of the Battee tribe, avoided the fury of the victorious enemy, by concluding a marriage between him and his daughter.

Sekander Khan was the only child he had by this lady. This chief does not appear to have entered into family connection with any of the Hindu chiefs. He married an Arab lady of his own tribe; by her he had Fatteh-ullah Khan, otherwise Tohel Khan, who succeeded him on his death.

Soon after Tohel Khan's accession, his principality was invaded by Rao Valoo, the chief of Brahmanabad, etc. His subjects were artfully gained over beforehand to the cause of the Rao, and thus an internal rebellion was raised, which compelled Tohel Khan to seek security by flight across the river Indus. He then fled towards Kerachee, and succeeded in dispossessing the Goojars of a tract of land; and here he built a town, which he named Kaher Beila.

Here he had a son, whom he named Pehla Khan, who inherited his estate on his death. This chief was more fortunate than his ancestor; and his affairs day by day assumed a more prosperous state. Many of the partisans of his father, who had been dispersed on his flight, again concentrated around his standard. On his death he was succeeded by Cheennee Khan, his son, who seems to have been also favoured by fortune. More of the neighbouring tracts of the country were subdued and added to the new principality. His party was greatly augmented by the arrival of numbers of fresh Arabs, Mekranees, etc., and in the short period, during which he had possessed the throne, every affair, owing to his prudent management, had taken a properous turn.

On the arrival at Multan of Shahzada Morad, the son of Akbar the Great, Cheennee Khan waited on him to pay his respects, and presented him at the same time with some rarities of the country. The prince was so much pleased with his insinuating manners, that he not only granted him a Jaghir, but conferred on him the title of Jam, which in the Sindh dialect means Chief. He was moreover entrusted with the collection of the government revenue from Sindh.

On his return, he appears to have settled at a distance of six coss from Sewistan, where he founded a new city, which he named Chekara Bazar. He extended his authority as far as Mekran on the west, and Marwar on the east. In short, his influence was so much increased, that his friendship was courted by all the neighbouring chiefs, among others by the chief of Kakrala, who was famous for his immense wealth and strength, and whose alliance secured him valuable presents.

The Ameer was very fond of shooting. The well-known hunting preserve called Odee was enclosed by this chief. It once happened that he mistook a man for an animal, and, taking a deliberate aim, inflicted a mortal wound on him. The poor man, in his dying agonies, solicited him to support his family, and the Ameer most generously and willingly agreed to do so; which promise he did not fail to keep.

Rana Dhora, the chief of Dhorang, seems to have drawn upon himself about this time the great resentment of the Ameer by some misconduct. Being however certain, that none but evil effects would arise from this, he purchased his forbearance by offering him the hand of his daughter. The nuptials were celebrated with unusual pomp and grandeur on either side.

By this marriage he had two sons: one named Mohammed Mehdee, and the other Daood Khan. According to one authority, the latter is stated to be the issue of the Ameer's alliance with the daughter of Sahoo Simma, his prime minister.

Cheennee Khan was remarkable for his peaceful disposition. His next act was to enter into a friendly alliance with the chief of Ganjaba, named Jam Pelanker. The ruins of a large pavilion erected by this prince to the west of that town are still to be seen. Besides the interchange of valuable presents in order to give steadfastness to their friendship, the two chiefs are said to have met together, according to appointment, on the banks of the river Boree. The feeling of cordiality thus established was mutually maintained by the two parties during their life.

The Ameer is said to have met his death by a strange accident. It happened that a half brother of his wife had been killed in an affray about a piece of water designed for the use of cattle. His sister was naturally much mortified; and in her great grief left her husband, and proceeded by water to her father's house. She was followed by the Ameer; but the boat in which he was sailing was accidentally broken by the kick of a horse, and consequently sunk suddenly with the Ameer. The year of his death is uncertain; but his age was one hundred and fifty. Mohammed Mehdee, his son, does not seem to have survived his father long, and the reins of government were therefore seized upon by Daood Khan, his younger brother. His succession was however strongly contested by Kohlara Khan, the son of his deceased brother, whose claims, perhaps from an opinion of his superior right, were supported by the leading people of the Abbasee party. A violent civil war appears to have broken out, when Daood Khan, having no possible hope of reconciliation, was obliged to retire, and take shelter with Vadeereh Jahankee Khan, of the Bakhawlee tribe, in the village of Denjsee, by whom he was received very hospitably. He was moreover allowed to occupy a piece of uncultivated ground, where he founded a village, and devoted himself to agricultural pursuits, the proceeds of which he alone enjoyed.

For three generations, his descendants appear to have lived by the same pursuits. Nothing worthy of notice is recorded of Mohammed Khan, his son, and Mohammed Khan, his grandson. The latter had a son named Daood Khan the second. He was endowed with extraordinary beauty, and was therefore appropriately named Chander Khan. He had many children, and lived to an age of more than two hundred years. It is from the circumstance of his extraordinary age, that he is called the "Great Grandfather;" and from him is derived the name of the Daoodputras (to which tribe the reigning family of Bahawalpur belongs). Bahadar Khan, son of Bhakar Khan, the son of Heibat Khan, the son of Saleh Khan, the son of Daood Khan, becoming straitened in his circumstances, was obliged to leave his native place, and proceeded to the town named Mada, in the vicinity of which he settled. Nothing further is mentioned of him. His grandson, Mohammed II., the son of Bhakar Khan, had three sons, namely, Arib, Firoz, and Esah. The well-known tribes of Arbanee, Firozanee, and Eshanee, take their origin from these three brothers. The elder, being given up to religious pursuits, left the management of his father's estate in the hands of Firoz. Hereafter, the latter seems to have quitted his paternal village, and to have proceeded to a place called Taraee, the chief village of the Cheena tribe.

Firoz Khan had five sons, the descendants of whom are traced out in the following table:—

FIROZ KHAN.

Vadeereh Jodeh Khan.			Bahadar Khan.		Kheirdeen Khan.		Omar Khan.	
Punnoo.	Jam.	Hoat.	Mobarik.	Kohneh Khan.	Balawul.	Abdulla.	Nanker.	Tamachee.

Bhakar Khan.				
Hotee.	Soobeh.	Taj Mohammed.	Shareef.	Samabeh.

DESCENDANTS OF KHALOORA.

BEFORE I resume the narrative of Daood Khan's descendants, it will be desirable to take a retrospective view of Khaloora Khan. It appears that, on the retirement of Daood Khan I., he did not survive long to enjoy his possessions. His state seems to have been divided, and to have fallen piece by piece into the hands of the neighbouring chiefs. History is silent about his descendants till 880 Hijra (1475, A. D), when Adam Shah, the ninth in descent from him, who led a monastic life, raised up a religious standard, and declared war against the local authorities of the Mogul emperor in Sindh. He carried on some warlike operation near Bhakar, where he was killed. His descendants are known by their religious character rather than by their political actions.

After this little digression, I must return to my story; and I shall here confine myself to the progenitors of the heroes of the above family of Bahadar Khan.

Firoz Khan was succeeded by his only son Bahadar Khan. He was remarkable for his conciliatory and engaging manners. On the death of Jalal Khan, the head of the Cheena tribe, he quitted Teraee, and proceeded towards Bhakar. Here he visited Nawab Mirza Khan, who governed the country on the part of the emperor Alamgeer, and succeeded in obtaining rent-free a sanud, or grant, of land in the neighbourhood. On this ground, he founded a town which was named Shikarpur.

He depended for his livelihood on agriculture, which he carried on with much care and prudence by artificial means of irrigation.

Unluckily, about this time, a difference occurred between the Ameer and the chief of the Lukhee tribe, which ended in the latter advancing upon Shikarpur with a large force. He was met by the Ameer in the field; and a most bloody action ensued between the two parties, when the Lukhee chief was totally routed, and compelled to seek safety in flight, whereby a large booty fell into the hands of the victors. The enemy was hotly pursued to the very walls of his capital, which was also successfully captured without much resistance.

Bahadar Khan, however, did not live long to enjoy the fruits of his victory. No date is given of his death, but he is said to have died soon after, and was succeeded by Mobarik Khan, his son.

Meanwhile Mirza Khan, the governor of the province, having died a natural death, his son was by royal order installed in his place. The rising prosperity of the Ameer attracted his jealousy, and he was not so favourably disposed as his father. This change of disposition in the governor alarmed the young chieftain. He endeavoured to restrain his anger through the interposition of Hamid Buksh, one of the descendants of the celebrated saint, Mohauddeen Gulanee of Uch. The saint proceeded in person to Bakhtyarpur, the town which the governor had lately built after his own name; but his councils and intercession had no effect on his mind.

The Ameer, apprehending an inevitable destruction by his further continuance at Shikarpur, was compelled to emigrate to the land inhabited by the Fatteh tribe. Here he erected a fortress, which afforded a shelter to his family, while he himself, with a strong body of three hundred chosen men consisting of the Khawaneens, or nobility of his tribe, proceeded to Multan. He was admitted to the presence of Shahzadà Moizuddeen, who received him with suitable attention. The Ameer tried his utmost to persuade the prince to cause the downfall of Bakhtyar Khan, his personal enemy, but did not succeed in his object.

In the meantime, the governor of Dereh, Ghazi Khan, rebelled against Shahzada; in consequence of which, the latter proceeded in person at the head of eight thousand troops to punish the rebel. He was met by Ghazi Khan in the field, and a severe contest ensued. At first the enemy gained some advantage over the royal troops, who were giving way. The Shahzada himself had a narrow escape; but, at last, the scale of victory was turned in his favour by the valorous exertions of the Ameer and his party, and the rebels were totally routed with great loss, both of killed and wounded.

While the two armies were engaged, Ghazi Khan detached a party of eight thousand men under two chosen commanders, to attack the harems of the Shahzada, which were left behind under the protection of some of the partizans of Mobarik Khan. The assailed party fought desperately, and repulsed the assailants with great slaughter.

The extraordinary bravery displayed by the young Ameer (who had hardly attained maturity) and his party in this war, raised him high in the confidence and estimation of the prince. He was exalted in rank, and moreover distinguished by the bestowal of other honors. The other Khawaneens of his party were also similarly honoured, and raised to the rank of Pansadee, or commanders of five hundred horse. Among others, Sangar Khan, who had acted very heroically in defending the harems, was honoured by the gift of a dagger personally used by the prince.

Having thus won the confidence of the prince, the Khawaneens took every opportunity of working on his mind, so as to cause the deposition of Bakhtyar Khan their common enemy. At last he yielded to their continued persuasion.

A party of troops under their command was detached to seize the ill-fated governor. They directed their movements with such quickness and secresy by unfrequented routes, that Bakhtyar was not aware of their advance until they suddenly made their appearance before Shikarpur. He was allured from his hold to a pitched battle in the open country. For sometime victory was doubtful; and many of the officers and men were slain on either side. At length Bakhtyar Khan himself coming in contact with one of the Khans, they fought hand to hand, when the former was driven *hors de combat*, and put to the sword. This circumstance decided the day in favour of the Khawaneens, and caused a general discomfiture and flight in the enemy's ranks. An immense and valuable booty fell into the hands of the victors.

The corps of Bakhtyar Khan was quartered by order of the prince to satiate his brutal revenge; and, as an example, a quarter was hung at the gateway of each of the towns of Shikarpur, Bakhtyarpur, Khanpur, and

Bhakar. It is asserted by some historians, that, on examination, the liver of Bakhtyar was found to weigh a quarter and a-half of a Seer, and was overgrown with hair, and that his feet were only half a span in length.

After the capture of Shikarpur, the prince was induced to make his public entry into the place. The Khawaneens were gratified with further honours, besides the grants of a Jaghir consisting of the villages attached to Shikarpur, and the towns of Bakhtyarpur and Khanpur. Moreover, they were entrusted with the general superintendence of the province and the fort of Bhakar.

In order to secure without dispute the succession of Sadik Khan, his son, Mobarik Khan, declared him his heir apparent, and invited all his nobility and officers to pay him public homage.

The rising prosperity of the Daoodputras excited the jealousy of the neighbouring contemporary chiefs; and with a view to check their further advancement, Meean Noor Mohammed Khan, of Khodabad, prepared a regular army to invade their principality. Meer Sehdad Khan, one of his chief officers, was detached in advance, and was soon followed by the chief in person. About 60,000 cavalry and infantry were collected at Larkana. When every warlike arrangement was complete, the unconditional surrender of Shikarpur and Khanpur was demanded; which request was of course at once rejected. Upon this, Noor Mohammed, reinforced by his allies, the chiefs of Lukhee, Moradkaleiree Khasa, etc., immediately proceeded to lay siege to Shikarpur, which city was not taken for some time. The besieged appear to have much annoyed the assailants by various sallies night and day. At length a breach was made in the southern wall of the fort. Despair gave courage to the besieged, and hence they defended the breach very vigorously. Much bloodshed was occasioned on both sides without any decisive result. At last, both parties being tired of the continuance of hostilities, mutual negotiations were commenced and concluded, through the mediation of the Lukhee chief, by which it was arranged that one half of the state was to be given up to Noor Mohammed, and the other half to continue in the possession of the Khawaneens. Thereupon the former raised the siege, and returned to his capital, leaving an officer to collect for him his share of revenue from the surrendered districts.

Scarcely six months had elapsed, when the cupidity of Noor Mohammed was again excited by the false reports of his collector, to complete his conquest of the Daoodputra possessions. A large force was again despatched under the command of Fatteh Khan Khaloora, to reduce Shikarpur. On his approach, he was met boldly by the Khawaneens, but succeeded in renewing the siege. As the fort was well defended, all his attempts to enter it were thwarted. The Khan, perceiving his incapacity to carry on the siege, a further reinforcement was detached to accomplish the object in view, but without any apparent success. Peace was therefore concluded; and the besiegers retired to Khodabad.

These unsuccessful operations, instead of discouraging Noor Mohammed, seem to have increased his sanguine expectations; for scarcely nine months afterwards, he detached a numerous force under his own brother, Mohammed Khan. A well contested struggle was the result, in which the enemy were put to great slaughter, and defeated by the Daoodputras.

This discomfiture very much provoked the still mortified Noor Mohammed. The next year he marched out personally with an immense force, far exceeding the last. About this time Mobarik Khan, the Daoodputra chief, suddenly died a natural death. This sad occurrence secured to his enemy peaceably what he could not gain by force. Sadik Khan, his successor, feeling his inability, on account of the weakness of his party, to hold the place, retired to the fort of Khanpur, whither he was immediately pursued. Not being able to keep his ground there, he retreated to a woody island in the neighbourhood, called Debli, without hazarding a battle; thus leaving the enemy in quiet possession of the whole territory, which he had inherited on the death of his father.

Noor Mohammed did not consider his conquest complete so long as the Daoodputra chief was at large. In order to exterminate his tribe, he prepared an armament consisting of twenty-eight boats, which he collected from Ghazi Khan of Dereh, and from Uch within a month. The Daoodputras were then attacked by water in their retreat; but they defended themselves with great bravery. Many of the chief officers of the enemy were drowned in the river, and several wounded, while the rest were repulsed with much slaughter, and fell back on Khodabad.

The forlorn condition to which Sadik Mohammed had been reduced, attracted the notice of his spiritual leader,

Sheik Abdul Kadir of Uch, and he was invited to take up his residence at that place. The invitation was readily accepted and forthwith acted upon. His progress, however, was checked by the turbulent tribes of Majhan, etc., etc., through whose country he passed. He, however, forced a passage and reached his destination in safety. The young chief was brought by the Sheikh under the notice of the governor of Multan, of the name of Shah Newaz Khan.

Sadik Mohammed accordingly proceeded to the latter place, and was received kindly by the governor. The Tallooka or district of Chodree was moreover conferred in perpetuity on him in Jaghir; and the Ameer consequently repaired thither to take possession of the grant, where he soon after founded a village, which was named Ilahabad.

The Daoodputras being beyond the reach of Meean Noor Mohammed himself, he now induced Rawul Akee Singh, the Jeyselmeer chief, to harass them in the best way he could. To oblige the Meean, the Rawul for that purpose sent out a party of his own men, who succeeded in carrying off their cattle while grazing in the jungle. This party was pursued by a foraging party, headed by Vadeereh Mand Khan; but they escaped without hurt, and the pursuers were obliged to return unsuccessful. In order to give a better colour to this incursion, the Rawul falsely represented to the Meean that the Vadeereh, who had made encroachments on the Jeyselmeer territory, had not only been repulsed, but was sent away with disgrace by submitting to a rope being put round his neck. Noor Mohammed, to taunt the bravery of the

Daoodputras, sent the original letter conveying the above intelligence for perusal to Sadik Mohammed. The Vadeereh was highly incensed at this false stain on his profession. The provoked Khan selected a party, consisting of the bravest men of his tribe, and forthwith proceeded to pillage the Jeyselmeer territory. He approached successfully to within two coss of that town; and he also succeeded in bringing away a number of mares belonging to the Rawul himself, but was chased and overtaken by a party of the Rawul's men, headed by his own brother Nahr Singh. A severe struggle was the consequence, when Nahr Singh and many of his party, fell prisoners into the hand of the Vadeereh, and were conducted to Chodree. To give an idea of the courage of his tribe, Sadik Mohammed Khan sent all the prisoners pinioned to Noor Mohammed.

In the meantime, the Lakhweira tribe had renounced allegiance to the emperor's government, and, having betaken themselves to open rebellion, infested the country to the very skirts of Multan. The Ameer was therefore desired by the governor to punish the rebels. Accordingly they were pursued by the Ameer, and put down in a short time. The town of Fareed was also captured and taken possession of by the Daoodputras. The governor was greatly satisfied with this service, and expressed his gratification in strong terms to the Ameer.

Availing himself of the occasion of the Ameer's absence in quelling the above insurrection, the Rawul of Jeyselmeer detached another party to attack his little principality. The whole Tallooka of Chodree, as well as the village Ilahabad and Uch, was completely pillaged, and a large booty fell into their hands and was carried away.

The Ameer watched for an opportunity to retaliate this unwarrantable outrage; and an incident soon occurred, which brought about what he wished. Kheir Khan, the chief of the Karkeich tribe, having received an injury at the hands of the Jonja people, who inhabited the forest, was anxious to take revenge. He consulted the Ameer how to proceed, and was advised by him to solicit the aid of the Jeyselmeer chief, who was on friendly terms with him. The Khan approved of the advice, and applied for assistance to the Rawul, who from a friendly regard complied with his request without any objection. The greater portion of his troops was accordingly detached with Kheir Khan to punish the Karkeich people. The absence of the Rawul's troops on this expedition presented the favourable opportunity Sadik Mohammed Khan sought for to attack and pillage his territory. He in consequence led his force in person, and at once laid siege to the fort of Deirawer, the pride of Jeyselmeer. The place was gallantly defended by the garrison; and the news of this invasion having meanwhile reached the force, it was detached along with Kheir Khan, who hastened his return, without accomplishing the object for which he had been sent, and directly proceeded to succour Deirawer. The Ameer, on receiving the intelligence of the approaching reinforcement, left the infantry to carry on the siege, while he himself advanced at the head of his cavalry, to prevent a junction of the enemy's troops. A severe struggle ensued; and two of the chief officers of the Rawul having fallen, it struck a panic throughout the whole force and caused a general flight, in which a great slaughter was committed among the fugitives. The victors returned to their entrenchments and doubled their exertions for the reduction of the place.

Beika, the prime minister of Jeyselmeer, who escaped with his life from the field, went on to Multan, while the governor was absent at Lahore. Owing to the latter's absence, he succeeded in tempting his deputy by some bribes, to aid him against the Daoodputras. With this succour the minister again advanced to make a diversion in behalf of the besieged; but he met with a second reverse. No sooner had he appeared before the place than he was boldly encountered by the besiegers, and repulsed with still greater loss both in men and property. The siege was now carried on with the greatest activity. At length a mine was run into the fort and exploded, which caused great destruction among the besieged. A general assault was then ordered through the breach, in which dreadful carnage occurred and very few escaped the fury of the victors; while among others eighteen of the officers of the enemy of high rank were put to the sword. Thus the fort of Deirawer was captured and occupied by the Daoodputras, in whose hands it has continued to this day.

At this time, Nadir Shah, the Persian monarch, having established his authority at Cabul, made his way through the Bengish country to Ghazi Khan of Dereh. As soon as Sadik Khan heard of his majesty's arrival at that place, he entrusted the superintendence of the fort of Deirawer to Vadeereh Mohammed, and without loss of time proceeded in person to tender his homage to that monarch, by whom he was received favourably. In the meantime, Noor Mohammed, hearing of his majesty's furious temper, avoided making his appearance, and confined himself in the fort of Amerkot. But it was not long before he discovered his mistake; for Nadir attacked him forthwith in the very same place, which he carried by assault, without meeting with much difficulty. The Meean fell a prisoner into his hands, and was conducted to the interior of Sindh, where, by making valuable presents, he succeeded in conciliating the monarch and purchasing his liberty.

Nadir now divided the province of Sindh into three parts. The district of Tatta with its dependencies was conferred on Noor Mohammed, who was at the same time distinguished by the title of Shahkolee Khan. The hilly part of the country was made over to the possession of Mahabut Khan, a Beloochee chief; while Shikarpur, Surkana, Sewistan, and Kachee, as far as the town of Choter, were given to the Daoodputras. At the same time, the latter were ordered to emigrate from Chodree, and to settle in the land of their forefathers, which was now restored to them.

As the affairs of this country had now become directly connected with the Persian court, the attendance of an agent on the part of the Daoodputras was considered a matter of great importance; and Sheikh Sadik, a man of great talents and of cultivated mind, was accordingly deputed by the Ameer to this duty. The Sheikh, by his expert and artful manners, soon gained some influence among the nobility of the court. But instead of employing it in favour of his master, he turned it to his own advantage. He succeeded in getting himself nominated to superintend the administration of the Bhakar states, while the superintendence of the Khalsa lands was made over to the charge of the Ameer.

As Nadir still entertained doubts regarding the attachment and fidelity of Noor Mohammed, he made him deliver over his sons, Mohammed Morad, and Gholam Shah, to remain as hostages for his future peaceable conduct.

After this, the monarch returned to Persia; the Ameer also soon after moved towards his restored territory, leaving his son Bahawal Khan, to continue in the present settlement.

The number of Daoodputras was now increasing daily; and, as it was considered necessary to settle them in proper places, lands were assigned to each respectively, on which they founded villages. Among others, Sangar Khan Bakhranee, Balawul Khan Firozanee, Ali Morad Khan Sangranee, as well as Bahadar Khan, Mullah Ali and Mohammed Maroof, were the first who laid the foundations of their villages. Bahawal Khan also founded a little town on the ridge of Tanwein, and Mohammed Khan Khamranee erected a fortress on the spot where the town of Bahawalpur now exists; while Kheirpur was founded by Maroof Khan. Thus severally settled, the Daoodputras employed themselves in agricultural pursuits; and their affairs flourished more and more every day.

Although Sheikh Sadik was under many obligations to the Ameer, he soon commenced interfering with his private affairs. To cause a disturbance, he unwarantably seized one of his subjects on the accusation of theft, and subjected him to many tortures. The prisoner, however, effected his escape from confinement, and took shelter with Sadik Khan. A party was then sent by the Sheikh to demand the fugitive. Although the Ameer suppressed his passion, yet some of the youths of his tribe could not brook the insult; and on the first impulse of resentment, forthwith proceeded to the residence of the Skeikh, and at once put him to the sword, together with his son, Akil, and some of his companions who attempted to save his life. The matter was immediately brought before the notice of his majesty by his surviving son, Fazil. Sadik Khan was naturally alarmed at the occurrence, and fearing that he should be severely called to account for the atrocity by the court, inflicted suitable punishment on the offenders; but, however, as a matter of precaution, he prepared himself to meet any misfortune. Under these circumstances, Bahawal Khan, together with Balawul Khan, was stationed at Skikarpur; and the fort of Keilah was made over to the charge of Abdullah Firozanee and Shah Mohammed Kehree. While the harems were removed under the charge of Mobarik and Fatteh Mohammed, the Ameer's younger sons, to Ilahabad, he himself proceeded to the Court, to represent the true state of the affair. But before he had reached his destination, Sirdar Tamasp, one of the chief officers of Nadir, having been chosen to retaliate the murder of Sadik, was already on his way to Shikarpur, with a chosen detachment of his majesty's troops. On the approach of the royal troops, Bahawal Khan removed all his valuables to the fort of Apara, while he himself retired to the fort of Deekampur, and a force was at the same time thrown into the fort of Deirawer under the command of some Khawaneens.

Balawul Khan, who thus remained alone at Shikarpur with a weakened garrison, found himself unable to defend the place; and was therefore compelled to evacuate it without offering any resistance, and to retire to a place called Sataha and situated in a forest subject to Jeyselmeer. Tamasp occupied the abandoned place without opposition, and siege was then laid to the fort of Keilah. Abdullah, the governor, however, considering it disrespectful to oppose the royal troops, threw himself on their mercy; upon which he was immediately made prisoner. This circumstance disappointed the garrison of their expectations of leniency from the besiegers; and they resolved upon death in preference to slavery. They first put their women to the sword, and next rushed out of the fort with sword in hand, and were most of them slain in desperate combat, while the rest made their escape to the forest.

Meean Noor Mohammed of Khodabad found the present a favourable opportunity to indulge his own malignant revenge against the Daoodputras, his old enemies. To furnish Tamasp with a plausible excuse for continuing his hostility to that tribe, he represented to him through his son, that they were guilty of usurping the Tallooka of Chodree from two brothers, who were loudly complaining in Multan, and that they deserved redress and restoration to their rightful inheritance. The Sirdar, who wanted such an excuse to gratify his resentment, lent a ready ear to the Meean's overtures. A consultation was forthwith held on the subject with Momin Khan, the governor of Multan, and Sheikh Rao of Seitpur, as well as with Nawab Jaunesar Khan of the Dereh of Ghazi Khan, who had already joined the royal force, which had now moved towards the latter place. It was resolved that the Sirdar should remain behind in the Dereh, while they themselves would advance against the Daoodputras along with the royal troops. The united forces accordingly proceeded to the strong hold of Deirawer, to which they at once laid siege. But, notwithstanding their vigorous exertions, they could not accomplish their object. At length, when all forcible attempts were frustrated, they hit on a stratagem. A person of great cunning, named Moosa, was selected to play the game. This man was formerly in the service of the Daoodputras, but was now in the employ of Noor Mohammed. He at once made his appearance in the fort, and pretending to have been deputed by Sadik Khan to deliver a message on the part of his absent master to the governor, Mohammed Maroof, stating that, as the Ameer already laboured under the displeasure of the court on account of the murder of Sheikh Sadik, it was not prudent to oppose the royal arms; and he was therefore requested to surrender the fort forthwith. At first, the sincerity of the messenger was doubted; but when he confirmed his assertion by a solemn oath on the Koran, any suspicion of his truth was removed. Accordingly, the unsuspecting governor, along with his chief officers, made his appearance in the camp of the besiegers, with a view to come to some favourable terms; when, to their great surprise, they discovered, too late to remedy, that instead of meeting a favourable reception as they were led to expect, they were all treacherously made prisoners.

The troops thus left without officers could not hold out any longer; but left the place, and retired to the woods, where they joined the rest of their tribe. The evacuated fort was garrisoned, and occupied by a party of Multan troops, and the prisoners, being at liberty, immediately joined their companions in the wood. Flushed with the success of their undertaking, they next pursued the Daoodputras to their retreat, headed by Tamasp in person. The Daoodputras, seeing no chance of escape, put to death all their women, and then with drawn swords fell upon the enemy. Great slaughter took place; and many of the officers of the royal forces fell victims to the resentment of their despairing enemies. At length, after a bloody conflict, the royal troops were totally routed. So terrible was their retreat through a sandy desert, that numbers of them died from wounds and fatigue on their way; while Tamasp himself reached Sindh with but few of his army remaining.

Meanwhile, the wretched condition to which the Daoodputras had been reduced, excited compassion at Nadir's Court, on account of their well-known bravery; and, in addition to this, Sadik Khan had interested a party in his behalf. He was soon restored to favour; Ghaznee with its dependencies was conferred on him in Jaghir, and he was dismissed with honours, accompanied by a royal officer named Mirza Askar Ali, to assist him in taking possession of his new Jaghir, and transferring his family and tribe thither. Accordingly, when the Ameer arrived at Shikarpur, he was welcomed on his approach by an officer on the part of Tamasp, and was received with every other suitable attention: while Meean Noor Mohammed at length setting aside his old enmity, proceeded to visit the Ameer at Loharee. Bahawal Khan, and the Khawaneens, who after the retreat of Tamasp on Sindh had resettled in the fortress of Chodree and Tanwein, were informed of the new arrangements which had been made in their behalf. In reply, they refused to submit to the terms, pleading that they had been subjected to various grievances at the hands of Tamasp, and that they considered the proposal of emigration, after so much suffering, an additional insult; and they advised the Ameer, therefore, to decline them, because they did not see any better prospects in removing to Ghaznee, but, on the contrary, expected that they would be entrapped into still greater difficulties. The advice thus offered by Bahawal Khan met with entire approbation from Sadik Khan; but, to quiet Askaree, he told him that he had written to his Khawaneens, to assemble for the purpose of removing to Ghaznee. At the same time he sent secret instructions to hold themselves in readiness for warlike operations. To give further colour to the plot, a letter was also received from Bahawal Khan, stating that he would, with the whole tribe, arrive for the above purpose at Shikarpur, within seven days. However, some of the friends to the royal party informed the Mirza that the preparations of the Daoodputras had more the appearance of hostility than of removal to Ghaznee. This intelligence alarmed the royal officer. To pay the Daoodputra chief in his own coin, he invited him to an entertainment, with a view to seize him on that occasion; but the Ameer was too cunning to be thus led away, and he therefore declined the proffered invitation. This failure obliged the Mirza to throw off the mask; and he accordingly proceeded openly to the fortress of Shikarpur, where Sadik Khan had shut himself up at the head of his party, with the avowed purpose of seizing him. His entrance into the place, however, was opposed by the Daoodputras; and a very bloody conflict was the consequence. Both parties maintained the battle with equal bravery; when, about midnight, some of the mercenaries, being disaffected, treacherously admitted the assailants into the fort from the northern and eastern gateways. The fight became exceedingly hot, and the loss of life on both sides was considerable. The women were as usual slain in the last extremity. Mohammed Sadik Khan, the Ameer, received a fatal wound, of which he almost instantly died; and eleven of his companions fell by his side. At the same time, Mobarik Khan, the son of the Ameer, was severely wounded; while those who escaped the sword, were obliged to effect their escape through the eastern gateway.

In the afternoon, Bahawal Khan arrived at the head of the Daoodputras, whom he had collected. Provoked by the death of his father, he immediately resumed hostilities without delay. Much bloodshed again occurred; but, at last, Askar Ali was put to flight. The last melancholy duties were then paid to the remains of the late Ameer, accompanied with every funeral honour; after which the bodies of the other victims were also collected and buried. No sooner, however, had Bahawal Khan gone through these ceremonies, than he hastened to attack Tamasp, who was quartered in a neighbouring fort. Both Tamasp and Asker Ali, feeling their inability to withstand him, sought safety in flight. It is stated, that Tamasp lost both his ears in this action; but according to others, in his flight in the woods. Whichever of these assertions may be true, it is difficult to determine; but it is certain that his ears were cut off in one or the other of these contests.

Bahawal Khan, though victorious, considered his position rather unsafe, and accordingly conducted his gallant tribe back to Chodree. On the road, he was molested by the hostile tribes who were attached to the royal cause, but from his vigorous conduct, succeeded in forcing his way, and returning safely to his own land.

Another bold actor now appeared on the stage, Koramul, a common Moherrer, or writer, was lately raised to the high office of deputy-governor of Multan, by the governor of that place. He was naturally an ambitious man. The governor, his own benefactor, now only stood in his way. To ease himself of this obstacle, he caused him to be perfidiously murdered in a squabble that was brought about through his means; and he then assumed the reins of government without resistance, under the title of Maharajah. To strengthen his position, he sagaciously endeavoured to make a combination with the neighbouring tribes. The Daoodputras, from their well-known bravery and chivalrous achievements, were the first who attracted his attention; and their friendship was easily secured through a constant correspondence with Bahawal Khan.

Meanwhile, Jaunesar Khan, the governor of Dereh Ghazi Khan, threw off the yoke of allegiance. Koramul was desired by the Moeenuddola, the Subah of Lahore, to bring the rebel to subjection; and the Maharajah solicited the aid of the Daoodputras in this expedition. Bahawal Khan, wishing for an opportunity of further distinguishing himself, readily assented, and forthwith put himself at the head of his troops, and effected a junction with the Maharajah at Tanwein, at which place he had arrived. Their united forces afterwards proceeded to attack Dereh, the province of Ghazi Khan. The operations were commenced by the capture of the fortress of Khanbeila, which fell without opposition. After this, their progress was checked by Jaunesar Khan in person. Petty skirmishes ensued, which lasted for three days. At last the rebel, unable to cope with the united forces, took advantage of night, and made his escape, leaving his army encamped on the banks of the Indus. Koramul was much gratified at the easy success of his army; but felt in a great measure indebted to the Daoodputras, and accordingly treated them with much favour and consideration.

After settling the country, and placing trusty men of his own party in the places of importance, the Maharajah retired to Multan, and Bahawal Khan to his own principality.

He now employed himself in ameliorating the condition of his country. Three new towns were built; viz.: Eastern Kheirpur, for Vadeereh Mohammed Maroof; Kaempur after Kaem-Khan; and Hasilpur so named after Hasil Khan, in consideration of their valuable services. Moreover Kaem-Khan was distinguished by the title of Raja; while Vadeereh Mohammed was directed to take possession of the entire district of Kheirpur, the income of which had been hitherto divided among many other Khawaneens. This last arrangement justly excited the jealousy of those who were deprived of their profits by it. Among those who raised their voices against the measure, were Vadeereh Mohammed Khan, Bahadar Khan, and Ikhtyar Khan, etc.; and to strengthen their faction, they persuaded Mobarik Khan, the younger brother of Bahawal Khan, to join them. This man, on account of some private differences, had been already disaffected. Their next step was to collect a force in the name of the young chief. When intelligence of these proceedings was brought to Bahawal Khan, he lost no time in bringing together his own scattered troops, and hastening at their head to Sohara, where he waited for the insurgents. The Ameer, being anxious to prevent the massacre of his own tribe, and much more to avoid fighting against his own brother, endeavoured to come to a reconciliation by various methods through his agents. At last, after a few days, he succeeded in separating him from the Vadeereh's party, upon which he granted him a free pardon, and restored him to favour.

The disturbance, however, continued. The insurgents, from a sense of their guilt, did not consider it prudent to trust the offended chief, however apparently disposed to forgive them. No sooner did they find themselves abandoned by Mobarik, than they filled his place by the selection of Ali Morad Khan Sanjranee as their head. Under him they moved to the western parts of the country; where they quietly settled themselves in various places. Bahawal Khan occupied Khandee, a large tract of uncultivated arable land which he brought under tillage. Ikhtyar Khan and some others entered his service as retainers on feudatory tenures. Ali Morad Khan also built a small town on the banks of the stream Dhoora, which he named Tarendeh; while Bahadar Khan Halanee, and Shebaz Khan, with his approbation, treacherously took possession of such tracts of land as they could lay their hands upon. The former founded the town of Bahaderpur, and the latter the village of Shehbazpur. The village of Mohammedpur is said to have been at the same time peopled by Vadeereh Mohammed Khan. Unity does not appear to have continued long among the new settlers, as several of them soon after returned to their own possessions, owing to the partiality of Ali Morad to those who were nearly connected with him. Among those who returned, the names of Hasil Khan, and Kaem Khan Khemranee, as well as of Shah Mohammed and Raja Mohammed Shawanee, who founded the Leidpur village, are mentioned. The Ameer received and treated them very kindly, which led to the return of many others. Among others, Mohammed Panah was treated with marked consideration. His village, named Kakh, was much increased in size, and is now called Bahawalpur. About the same time, to secure the protection of the Moreaba tribe, the Ameer built a fortress, about thirty koss distant in the woods; which was named Majghur. While he himself was thus engaged in improving his settlement by personal exertions, his example had a desirable effect on his people. Ahmed Khan, the son of Khader Khan, on the death of his father, built a large town, the ruins of which are to be seen to this day, to the west of the present Ahmedpur. To supply the deficiency of water, he cut the canal named Khanwa from the Gara (the Sutlej is here known by this name), which amply supplied with this necessary both men and animals, while there was also a sufficiency for agricultural purposes.

Koramul, the governor of Multan, who is already mentioned as having been much gratified by the valorous conduct of the Daoodputras, in order to prove his estimation of them, granted a perpetual lease to Bahawal Khan, of the Adam Wahen Tallooka. The Ameer took every measure to improve his new acquisition, and moreover dug through it the canal Shahdurra, which considerably fertilised the whole tract of country.

While Bahawal Khan was thus peaceably enjoying the fruits of his labours, and zealously devoting his time to furthering improvements, he was suddenly attacked by rheumatism, which soon put an end to his existence. He died in A.H. 1163 (A.D. 1749), leaving no issue.

Mobarik Khan, his younger brother, succeeded. He occupied the vacant Musnud without resistance; and his succession was peaceably acknowledged at home as well as abroad. He was also recognised by the governor of Multan, who deputed agents to condole with him for the death of the late Nawab, and to congratulate him on his undisputed succession.

The first thing that engaged the notice of the present chief, was the incursion of the Mareeja tribe, who, during the illness of the late Khan, had wrested the fortress of Morat from his people. As soon as he had secured his succession, he sent out a force under the command of Vadeereh Mohammed Maroof, to expel the foresters. They, however, were met by the Mareejas outside the walls, and a severe struggle ensued. The Mussulmans drove them to the foot of the fort, and at last compelled them to surrender at discretion, while the fort was recovered and re-occupied without further resistance. The Khan was much gratified on hearing the intelligence, and celebrated this first act of his reign by giving feasts and entertainments.

The young chief, like his brother, was naturally disposed to agricultural habits. After the expulsion of the Mareejas, his next act was to purchase the tract of land named Shahnee Bakhree and Madawala, from the Sheikh Rajoo, and to have it connected with his own principality. At the same time, he divided the western land of the suburbs of Bahawalpur into many divisions, which he bestowed on his relations. He also built a town about the same period, which he named after himself Mobarikpur.

Ahmed Shah Durranee, taking advantage of the revolution which occurred on the death of Nadir Shah, declared himself the ruler of Khorasan. Ali Mohammed Khan, who rented Dereh, the district of Ghazi Khan, on the part of the new government, being originally ill-disposed towards the Daoodputra chief, took every opportunity to calumniate him; and at last induced his majesty to despatch Sirdar Jahan Khan against him. On his arrival at the Dereh, he was met by Jaunesar Khan, of Multan, who, having obtained an insight into his views, communicated the same to Mobarik, with whom he was on friendly terms. In the meanwhile, the Sirdar moved to Uch, while the Khan, instead of opposing his progress, took shelter in the fort of Majghur, which was situated in the woods to the south of Bahawalpur. At the same time, Vadeereh Mohammed threw himself into fort of Morat, and some other Khans into the newly-built one of Bholreh. Orders were also issued to all the rest of the Khans of the tribe to assemble forthwith at Kheirpur, where they would be joined by Mobarik. The Khans accordingly, in obedience to the orders of their superior, assembled together in the place above named, and reported their arrival to the latter, who, without loss of time, leaving the females of the family at Majghur, proceeded thither at the head of about a thousand Sawars, or horsemen, with the chief Khans in attendance. The enemy meanwhile moved to Bahawalpur, and lost no time in sending out a force, amounting to about eight thousand men, towards Kheirpoor, to surprise the Daoodputras. Mobarik Khan, who closely watched their motions, also moved out of his encampment at Kheirpur; and the two armies came into collision at Khatala, about two koss distant to the west. A severe contest ensued; the enemy were completely routed, and compelled to fly. They were followed as far as Sohara, where the pursuit was given up.

Considering the time favourable, Mobarik Khan soon began to make overtures of peace to the enemy, who listened to them with a ready ear. Peace was concluded on very favourable terms, through the agency of an ambassador, when Jahan quitted Bahawalpur, and crossing over the Sutlej at the ferry of Fattehpur, bent his course towards Multan, whence he proceeded to Khorasan by way of Jung Seyala.

On the morning of Wednesday the 27th of Safer, 1166, A. H. (A. D. 1752), Fatteh Mohammed, the third son of Mohammed Sadik Khan, was favoured by the birth of a son, who was named Jaffer, afterwards Bahawal Khan the Second. By a singular coincidence, the intelligence of the death of Noor Mohammed, the chief of Sindh, was received on same day. Mobarik Khan having had no issue, looked upon his cousin from the beginning as his successor, and treated him accordingly.

The friendship existing between Nawab Jaunesar Khan and Mobarik now received additional strength, in consequence of the Nawab's having regained, in the year 1167 (A. D. 1753), the government of Multan: in the management of which, he asked the assistance of his friend. Mobarik Khan accordingly proceeded thither personally, and materially assisted the governor, in introducing a reform; but his own affairs demanding his early attention, he hastened his return. However, he was soon recalled, and employed in completing the reform, which he succeeded in accomplishing to the great satisfaction of his friend.

On his return from Multan, the Khan fixed upon Bahawalpur as the seat of his government. About this time, the town of Kheirpur was built by Balawul Khan, and named after Kheir Mohammed, his cousin. This individual emigrated from Khoandee to Bahawalpur in the reign of Bahawal Khan the Great, when a piece of land was given to him within eight koss of that town on which he settled. Through his energetic exertions, he brought the whole land under cultivation; and hence his affairs wore a prosperous aspect, which enabled him to build the town in question. Besides this, he cleared out a canal, which had been made in the time of Aurungzeb, the Mogul emperor; but had for many years remained neglected and choked with rubbish. It was on Balawul Khan's emigration from Khoandee, that it fell into the hands of Hojee Ikhtyar Khan, who took great pains in improving his new possession. He also dispossessed of his fort, Shadee Khan, one of the dependents of Noor Mohammed, who had settled there, and the place was converted into his residence, and named after himself.

In the commencement of 1170, A. H. (A.D. 1756), Jaunesar Khan having been killed in one of Ahmed Shah's expeditions against Hindustan, his son, a child of four years old, named Allahdad Khan, was generously appointed by his majesty in the room of his father, while Burkhurdar Khan, his cousin, was nominated guardian and regent during his minority. He was not, however, equal to the responsible duties with which he was entrusted; for he turned out to be a great spendthrift, and indiscreetly brought the revenues of the state into a very embarrassed condition. The matter was brought to the notice of Sheikh Rajoo, the son-in-law of the late Nawab, who pleaded his cause from a due regard to the interests of his young relative. Accordingly, he proceeded in person towards the Dereh, at the head of a large Beloochee force, with a view to check the irregularities of the indiscreet manager. On the arrival of the Sheikh, Burkhurdar saw his own ruin imminent. He therefore marched out with a force to prevent the approach of the Sheikh. The two parties encountered each other near a village named Jampur; and a conflict ensued, in which Burkhurdar was totally defeated, and obliged to take shelter with the Mukdoom Saheb of Uch. The administration of the affairs of Allahdad was now entrusted by the victorious Sheikh, to the hands of his able private minister, Ahmed Khan, a person considered the well-wisher of his young ward, from his having been in the service of his late father.

The object of Burkhurdar, in going over to Uch, was to make the Mukdoom Saheb, another son-in-law of the late Nawab, and who was already well-disposed and still further interested in his behalf, in which point he succeeded. The Mukdoom was moved with pity at his deplorable condition, and lost no time in deputing one of his chief officers to Mobarik Khan, to sue for the aid of an army in his behalf. The Khan could not resist the demand of his spiritual leader; and forth with proceeded in person with a few of his nobles to Uch, where, according to his order, he collected his troops from the eastern and western parts of his territory. In the year 1171 (A.D. 1757), he marched out to recover the Dereh of Ghazi Khan for the Burkhurdar. He was met at some distance from the town by Ahmed Khan, when a battle ensued, which was fought desperately on both sides for some time; but in the midst of the conflict, Ahmed Khan having been slain, his troops took to flight. The young Nawab, who was sitting in a palanquin, was captured alive, and brought to the presence of Mobarik, who delivered him over in an appropriate manner, to the custody of the Burkhurdar, accompanied with wholesome advice how to treat him, and to manage his affairs in future. After completing all these satisfactory arrangements, the Khan returned to his own capital crowned with success.

About this time, Bahadar Khan Allanee, an enterprising and ambitious character, following the advice of a Hindu of Jeyselmeer, ventured to sink a well in the Kobistan, or woods, which fortunately produced sweet water. This circumstance induced the adventurer to erect a Burj, or bastion, near the well. He was, however, opposed in its construction by the Jeyselmeer chief; but ultimately succeeded in finishing it, to the great alarm of that prince. The place was named Deengurh.

On the death of Noor Mohammed Khaloora of Sindh, he was peaceably succeeded by his son, Mohammed Morad, who continued in the enjoyment of absolute authority for nearly five years. He was naturally of a violent temper, which disgusted his nobles, and provoked them against him. The consequence was, that he was put in confinement, and his brother, Gholam Shah, raised in his stead to the vacant throne. In the meantime, while matters were thus going on at home, Ater Khan, the third brother, succeeded in the court of Ahmed Shah in getting himself nominated to succeed his father, and with a royal reinforcement, commanded by Hajji Ataee, arrived at Shikarpur about this time to carry out his design. His approach was sufficient to shake the authority of the newly exalted chief, who was soon deserted by his troops, and obliged, after a reign of only six months, to seek safety in flight towards Jeyselmeer and Beekaneir. The few of his adherents who accompanied him in his escape, also fell off one by one until he reached Jeyselmeer. Soon after his arrival here, he sent a deputation to Mobarik to solicit his aid in support of his cause. As a preliminary course to negotiation, he was advised by the Daoodputra chief to move to Majghur, his own fort. Gholam Shah readily complied with the request, and forthwith proceeded thither. About this time, the Khan also happened to be there on some private business. The ex-chief was received with every due honour and respect, was met on his approach by Fatteh Khan, the Khan's own brother, conducted to the place with proper ceremonies, and on arrival was treated very hospitably by the Khan himself. Soon after, on the return of the latter to Bahawalpur, Gholam Shah also accompanied him thither.

While the exile had thus secured the favour of the Daoodputra chief, fortune was not backward in favouring his cause at home. No sooner had Ater Khan taken possession of the Musnud, than he abandoned himself to indolent pleasures and luxuries, and totally neglected his affairs. His conduct provoked the nobles, who soon grew anxious to get rid of him. The best contrivance they could devise, was to open negotiations for recalling the ex-chief, Gholam Shah, who most readily accepted this voluntary invitation. To enable him to return, he solicited the assistance of his host; and a force was accordingly prepared under the command of Fatteh Khan to support his cause. Some mercenaries were also gathered together by the latter from Multan and the neighbouring towns. The combined troops soon after proceeded on the expedition against Ater Khan. On hearing of the approach of his rival, the latter was roused from his lethargy, and with his brother, Ahmed Yar, boldly met him in the field. A very severe conflict ensued; many of Ater Khan's party were killed; and among the rest, Hemza, the brother of Raja Lukhee, the chief of Beloochistan; this accident completed his discomfiture, and compelled him to fly, leaving his victorious enemy in the possession of the whole territory. The Daoodputra troops having now accomplished their object, returned to Bahawalpur.

An anecdote, which is recorded of Gholam Shah in this action is very creditable to his character, in point of morality. It is stated, that in the heat of the battle, an individual named Behram deserted to his side, fully expecting to meet with a favourable reception for his conduct; but he was quickly undeceived. As soon as he appeared before Gholam Shah, the latter, in order to remind him of his disloyal conduct, offered him a loud Salamo-alik, meaning to show that he did not approve of his treacherous desertion. The man was ashamed, and hung down his head.

Ater Khan, with his brother, proceeded in his flight towards Candahar, but he was interrupted and seized on his arrival at Kelat, by Nasir Khan, the chief of the place. His liberation, however, was afterwards effected through the exertions of his own agent, a Hindu, in the court of Ahmed Shah. He was, moreover, sent back to Sindh with a fresh reinforcement of royal troops, with which he soon arrived in the country.

As the country had already suffered much from civil war, the nobility, with a view to prevent further bloodshed, advised the two brothers to divide the territory among themselves. Accordingly, Tatta, with all its dependencies, was given to Gholam Shah, and Khudabad and Ahmedabad, as far as Sohara, were made over to Ater Khan; but after some time, the former dispossessed him again of his division by some artful stratagem. Upon this, Ater Khan quickly settled in the fort of

Ikhtyar Khan, while his brother, Ahmed Yar, proceeded to Hindustan.

In the year 1173, A. H. (A.D. 1759), Rao Sing, the chief of Jeyselmeer, having demolished the old bastions of the fort of Deirawer, and replaced them with new ones, moved to that place with his family, and made it his residence. Khawaja Rahmet, the officer who commanded the garrison on the part of the Multan governor, also occupied one side of the fort, with a portion of the troops, while the rest of his men were quartered without the walls. The duties levied on the transit trade were henceforward equally divided between him and the Rawul. The latter, however, dreaded the daily increasing prosperity of Mobarik, and did not consider himself safe, without securing the friendship of that chief. With this view, he opened negotiations with the Mukdoom Saheb of Uch, and succeeded in purchasing his alliance by voluntarily delivering over the fort of Deirawer, on condition of receiving a certain amount of money in lieu of it for himself and his colleague, the Khawaja. The fort was further strengthened by the Khan, with some additional improvements to the fortification. Leaving this place from motives of policy, Mobarik moved in the direction of Fatteh Fareed, and succeeded in occupying the fort of Anoopgerh.

A letter was about this time received from Gholam Shah, the Sindh chief, complaining, that, notwithstanding the great friendship which existed between himself and the Khan, his rebellious brother, Ater Khan, was assisted by Bahadar Khan Allanee, one of his dependants, in making preparations to renew hostilities against him, and soliciting the Khan's interference in preventing his design. Mobarik Khan in consequence advised Bahadar Khan, through the medium of some other Khans, to desist from his mischievous purpose, but he turned a deaf ear to all his counsel; and Gholam Shah was therefore obliged to take the field, with a numerous force at Meerpur, in order to meet the rebellious troops which were in force in that direction. The two parties came in contact near the village of Obawra, and a severe conflict ensued. As Gholam Shah was encouraging his troops, he was seen by Bahadar Khan, who hastened to surprise, and kill him. But before he could approach him, he was met with a volley of musquetry from the Meean's men, in which both he and his horse were each struck with two balls, and fell dead instantly. His head was immediately severed from his body, and presented to Gholam Shah; at the sight of which, Kabeir Khan, the brother of the deceased, an old servant of the Meean, who was standing behind his master, appeared much dejected. The Meean was accordingly moved with compassion, and delivered over the head and body of the deceased to his brother. Vadeereh Mohammed, and some other chiefs of note of Ater Khan's party were also killed at the same time, and several of them were wounded. He, himself, and those who escaped the slaughter, were obliged to seek safety in flight; and, by way of Bahawalpur, they safely reached Gurkee Ikhtyar Khan.

About this period, the attention of Mobarik was engaged by the rebellion of some of his nobles. It is stated, that, in the time of Bahawal Khan the Great, Morya, a Daoodputra, had reinhabited a place situated in the desert, which had been the residence of a famous woman, named Maroe, after whom the Marwar country is named, and where various stories of her are sung. An old well was also repaired by him in this place. Being under no immediate control, he commenced exacting duties on commerce at four anas per camel. His success excited the cupidity of another Daoodputra chief, named Ali Morad, who also dug a well, and constructed a bulwark close to Morya's settlement. The Khan also erected a castle there; but made over the superintendence of his possession to Morya.

Ali Morad was naturally displeased at this new settlement, and evinced some rebellious designs towards his own master. He was in consequence attacked by Mobarik Khan, deprived of his possession, and expelled from it along with his family. Between the two bulwarks above named, the Khan built a fort on the site of a fortification, which had been constructed by a Kafir, or infidel, named Ranja, and demolished by Ala-uddeen Ghoree. This fort was called Ranjroot.

Some of the Khemranee and Kheranee people, on the instigation of some of the nobles, had also evaded the payment of the government dues; but they were soon quieted by persuasive means, and were mercifully pardoned for their past conduct.

This period of Mobarik's reign is particularly remarkable for the arrival of ambassadors from Hindustan and Khorasan, together with some learned men; and it is also noted for the despatch of agents to Multan, the Dereh, and to the court of Ahmed Shah. The strength of the standing army was also numerically augmented.

The Khan himself about this time resided towards Eastern Mobarikpur, and Tatta Fareed, while Laldas, one of his old and attached slaves, superintended the civil affairs at Bahawalpur; and, by his experienced management, greatly improved both the place itself, and also the surrounding district. The Khan also improved the cultivation of the lands situated on the right bank of the Sutlej, by facilitating the means of irrigation, and by cutting the canals of Mobarikwah, Naneewah, Sardarwah and Khanwah, etc. Numbers of cultivators and tradesmen, especially the peasantry of Multan, who were severely oppressed by Ali Morad, the governor, took refuge in the Bahawalpur territory.

The sons of the late Noor Mohammed of Sindh, named Gholam Nabee, and Abu Nabee, at this time threw themselves on the hospitality of the Khan. They were received and treated with every proper mark of respect and consideration.

The fortification of Anoopghur had much alarmed the mind of Jey Singh, the chief of Bikaner. As long as the place remained occupied by the Daoodputras, he did not think his own frontier safe; neither did he consider himself powerful enough to cope with his antagonist without foreign help. He therefore applied for aid to the Jypur and Jodhpur chiefs; but they both expressed their inability to comply with his request: the former on account of the great distance, and the latter from the friendly alliance which then existed between himself and the Daoodputra chief. Jey Singh, therefore, failing in obtaining reinforcements from either quarter, proceeded to do what he himself could. He at once despatched all his troops under the command of one of his chief functionaries, by name Moolchund, to lay siege to the fort. No sooner had he appeared before the place, than he was boldly opposed by the garrison; and much bloodshed occurred on both sides. At last the invaders were repulsed, and obliged to retreat.

Jey Singh was not, however, discouraged by the failure of this expedition; but threw himself on the support of Gholam Shah, the Sindh chief. The latter did not apparently favour his cause; but, in reality, turned the matter to his own advantage. About this time, Ater Khan, the ex-chief of Sindh, had employed his influence in the court of Ahmed Shah, in having an order issued to Meer Hazar Khan, who had succeeded Ali Morad in the governorship of Multan, to capture Sindh for the king. Wishing to avail himself of the opportunity, Ater Khan went over to Multan; but as he did not meet with the reception he expected, he was obliged to come back to the Gurhee of Ikhtyar Khan. Notwithstanding the Khan remonstrated against his stay there, no attention was paid to his requisition by Ikhtyar Khan. Gholam Shah, however, did not appear satisfied at the apparent remonstrances of Mobarik Khan, and accordingly complained against him to his majesty, Ahmed Shah; and in the year 1174 Hijra (1760, A.D.) he succeeded in obtaining orders under the names of the governors of Multan and the Dereh, to co-operate with him in reducing the rebellious Ater. Hereupon the Sindh chief proceeded in person with a large force to punish his enemy. The latter, however, as well as his host, Ikhtyar Khan, feeling their total inability to meet him in the field, retired to the fort of Deirawer, where they received a ready shelter from the Daoodputra chief. This circumstance gave further cause of complaint to the Sindh chief against Mobarik. He never ceased making direct overtures; and demanded the delivery of Ater Khan through the Mukdoom Saheb of Uch. The Khan, however, upon reflection, did not think it either honourable or creditable to himself, to deliver up a person who had taken refuge under his protection; and accordingly tried to pacify the provoked Gholam Shah, by sending him some suitable excuses.

After the settlement of this affair, the Khan moved to Mobarikpur, where he succeeded in reducing Mohammed Azeem Khan to subjection. Shaker Fareed of Pakpatan was also attacked, and some lands in that quarter were brought into the possession of the Khan.

After this, Mobarik commenced building the fort of Sirdarghur; but the construction of it was hindered by the Bikaner chief, who, when he saw that remonstrances were vain, sent out a force of about ten thousand horse and footmen, assisted by some nobles of the Jodhpur territory, to prevent the completion of the fort. On their approach, they were met by the Daoodputra troops, headed by some officers of rank. A severe contest ensued, in which the enemy were repulsed, with great loss; and the fort was afterwards finished without any obstruction.

About this time, the attention of the Khan was attracted by the sudden irruption of the Sikhs, and the people of the Omeira tribe, who were notorious for their predatory habits. They were, however, soon reduced to obedience without much trouble. But new and more powerful enemies now appeared on the stage (1180, Hijra, A. D. 1766). Jhunda Singh, Gunda Singh, and Haree Singh, the Sikh chiefs, who had lately disturbed the tranquillity of the Punjaub, proceeded with a numerous force to fight their Mohammedan foe, and encamped on the right bank of the Sutlej. The Daoodputras could not endure the sight of them, but crossed the river, and provoked them to a pitched battle, which was maintained with great severity on both sides. At last the operations terminated by the conclusion of a treaty, in which it was stipulated that, in future, Pakpatan was to form a mutual frontier; and that neither potentate was to encroach within the boundaries of the other.

Ikhtyar Khan Mundhanee, who was proud of the occupation of a stronghold in Kohistan, was naturally disposed to extend his possessions. In the year 1191, A. H., (A. D. 1777), he persuaded the officer in charge of the fort of Jahar, belonging to Jeyselmeer, to give him over the keys of the place; and by this treacherous means he took possession of the fort, which he named Islamghur. The traitors were rewarded by him with Khelats and gilt bangles.

A fort was also erected about this period by Ibrahim, the son of Vadeereh Mohammed, to the west of Majghur. It was named Deenghur.

Towards the end of the above year, Ali Mohammed was restored to the government of Multan, while the province of Dereh was placed under the management of Sirboland Suddoozye, on the part of Ahmed Shah. He was a man of weak character; and as the reports of the decline of the Suddoozye power were at this time abroad,

Ali Mohammed availed himself of the opportunity, and being assisted by the Daoodputra chief, dispossessed the new governor of the Dereh territory, and divided his acquisitions equally between himself and Mobarik, as a recompense for his valuable aid. The Ilakas, a district of Khanwa, etc., situated on the right bank of the river, was also leased to the Khan for eight thousand rupees annually; and besides this, the lands of the Meilsee tribe, which had been captured by Mobarik during the above military operations, and had been made over by him to the charge of Jam, the son of Mullah Ali Kehranee, were conferred on him in perpetuity, in consideration of his services. The tenure on which they were given was in perpetual farm; and according to the lease he was to pay four hundred rupees yearly. A strong fort was built on this ground, and was named Meilseeghur. A Nullah was also dug for the purposes of irrigation, and was called Ali, after the name of the father of the founder.

Among other outrages committed by Ali Mohammed since his restoration, he had seized the person of Nawab Shuja Khan Suddoozye, and had thrown him into confinement. This proceeding had incensed his Durranee majesty to a high decree, and when, in 1181 (A. D. 1767), the Shah returned from his expedition against Hindustan towards Multan, the governor, apprehending a severe retribution from his justly provoked master, removed all his valuables and females to Majghur, where he placed them under the custody of Mobarik, while he himself left his son, Sokhee Khan, in charge of his government, and proceeded directly to the court of his friend, to consult him as to which was the best course to adopt in the present emergency. The Khan told him, that the chief cause of his majesty's irritation was the apprehension of Shuja, and that his appearance alone would still more excite the fiery temper of his majesty. He therefore advised him to set his prisoner at liberty, to give him every satisfaction by making amends for what he had done, and through his interposition to obtain pardon for himself. Ali Mohammed was too proud of his own abilities and valuable services, to take this wholesome advice; and, on the approach of the monarch, at once made his appearance in court. He was, as had been expected, immediately seized, together with his son, and their bellies were ripped open by order of Ahmed Shah. Their corpses were put on camels, and paraded throughout the town of Multan; and a proclamation was at the same time made, declaring that any one who should presume in future to shew disrespect to the Suddoozye people, would meet with a similar fate.

Shuja Khan was soon liberated, and invested with the government of Multan, while the management of the Dereh was added to the charge of Gholam Shah of Sindh, through the good offices of Dewan Kuddomul.

It has been already stated, that Mobarik had no issue; for which reason he always treated Jaffer, his nephew, with great affection. As he was naturally endowed with high merit, and a nobility of mind, the Khan fixed upon him as his heir apparent, and with that view gave him a liberal education by employing learned teachers for that purpose. The young man soon made very great progress in literature, and gave early proofs of his good disposition and talents. In 1183 (A. D. 1769), his marriage was celebrated with the daughter of Kohneh Khan, the son of Bahadar, the son of Kohneh Khan, the head of the Firozanee tribe.

In the commencement of 1185 (A. D. 1771), the Sikhs, to the number of about one hundred thousand, and commanded by Gunda Singh, made an irruption into the Multan territory, and from thence carried their plundering incursions into the country of the Daoodputras. Jaffer Khan was in consequence sent out to expel them; and a severe battle ensued. The Daoodputras behaved very gallantly; many of their officers were killed; and they might have lost the day, had they not been reinforced in time by the arrival of fresh troops sent by Mobarik. The fight then became hotter; but Majja Singh, the commander of the Sikhs having been struck dead by a ball, his followers fled from the field; while the young Daoodputra chief, flushed with his first victory, returned to the capital.

Towards the end of the year, the bravery of Jaffer was again put to the test. Ikhtyar Khan Mundhanee having rebelled, had forcibly occupied some Khalsa or crown lands, as well as some belonging to a nobleman. And in consequence of this, the young chief was deputed to bring him to subjection. The rebel at first showed some disposition to oppose Jaffer, but being deserted by his partisans, he immediately threw himself on his mercy and humbly begged forgiveness, which was generously granted.

About this time, Ahmed Shah died of a disease in his nose, which penetrated into his brain, and he was succeeded by his son Timur.

It is stated, that in the end of the same year, Meean

Gholam Khaloora also met with a mysterious death. He was engaged in building the fort of Hyderabad; in the course of which he ordered the remains of some dead bodies to be removed, when he was suddenly shot dead by a pistol-ball; but the discharger of the pistol was never seen by any one. He was succeeded by Surfaraz Khan, his son. Mobarik Khan's life also terminated about this period. He had, for some time, been afflicted with a retention of urine; and the complaint had so much increased since the latter part of Safer, 1186 (A.D. 1772), that he died in the ensuing month of the same year.

ACCESSION OF BAHAWAL KHAN II.

MOHAMMED JAFFER, who had already been recognised as heir apparent by his late uncle, ascended the throne with the consent of his own father as well as of all the nobility, and henceforward assumed the name of Bahawal Khan. As soon as the ceremonies of the accession were over, Mobarik Khan was buried with the usual rites in the family cemetry by the side of Bahawal Khan the First. A few days after his elevation, the new chief was favoured by the birth of a son, who was named Wahid Buksh, otherwise Mobarik Khan. He was born on the 1st of Rabeeussanee 1186 (A. D. 1772).

The authority of Bahawal Khan was acknowledged by all the Khans without the least opposition; while the chief, on his part, treated them with consideration, and promoted some of them to high rank. Vadeereh Jan Mohammed, one of the principal chiefs, along with his brother Noor Mohammed, was selected to fill the office of Vizir, or prime minister; while Islam, Shah Mohammed, Sheikh Bahar, Soneh, Deir Mohammed, and Gholam Hussain, together with Sultan Mohammed, Bader Ali and Kehram Mehr, were nominated as private counsellors. The situation of Mukhtaree was also conferred on Dewan Laldas, an old servant of the state. About this time Meer Kazim Ali and Meer Buksh Ali, who were the chief managers of the affairs of Hussun Ali Khan, and Abd-ullah Khan of Bahra, owing to the decline of the Mogul empire, arrived at Bahawalpur. They were employed by the young chief as his preceptors, and were also generally admitted into his councils.

Bahawalpur was now considered a place of the greatest security. The disorder and anarchy occasioned throughout India by the dismemberment of the Mogul empire, on the one hand, and the declining power of the Khorasan monarchy on the other, induced several respectable families to settle at this place for safety. Among others, Gungardher, who, from his personal merit, had obtained the situation of Dewan under the Mahrattas on their sallying forth to Multan, arrived thence with his three sons; while Alladad, the son of Jaunesar, Said Daem Shah, and Dowaramul Dewan also arrived from Dereh Ghazi Khan. The sudden rise of the Sikhs in the Punjaub also obliged many respectable Mullahs and Mohammedans, such as Molwees Fazul Islam and Hafeezul Islam, as well as three other great Molwees, etc. to emigrate to Bahawalpur. Hafeezul Islam was employed by the Khan to instruct him in "Tufseir and Hadeis," or the Commentary and Wise Sayings.

Surfaraz Khan Khaloora, the chief of Sindh, one of the bitterest enemies of the late Mobarik Khan, now left his capital, apparently on a trip of pleasure to the Derehjats, but really to have a meeting with Bahawal Khan, with a view to have a better insight into his affairs, in order that he might be enabled to cause a disturbance in the Bahawalpur state. On his way he was met by Mukdoom Sahib Sheikh Hamed of Uch, with whom he had a private interview, in which he disclosed his design. The Mukdoom undertook to accomplish this object on the payment of two lakhs of rupees, namely, one lakh for the purpose of building a fortification round Uch, and the other lakh as a contribution for his services. When matters were thus arranged, the Mukdoom employed himself in effecting a meeting between Bahawal Khan and Surfaraz Khan, which was soon arranged through the agency of Vakeels. The meeting accordingly took place between the two potentates, and during it much friendly conversation passed between them. In the course of this conversation, a verse escaped the Sindh chief while looking at the face of Bahawal Khan. It is this:—"Where is the limit to the beauty of which I yet only see the beginning." At the same time, Surfaraz had a private conference with the Mukdoom, in which they consented to foment a disturbance among the nobles of Bahawal Khan. With this view, they treated Ikhtyar Khan and Noor Mohammed Marufanee, the prime ministers, as well as some other chiefs, in a very conciliating manner. Besides this, several of them were soon after assembled by the Mukdoom in a temple at Uch, where he spoke largely of his own religious character, and delivered a long harangue on the liberality of the Sindh chief. The Koran was then produced, and he called on those present to take an oath of attachment to that chief. Among the rest, Noor Mohammed bound himself by a solemn oath to follow the advice of the religious leader. Bahawal Khan was not ignorant of the disloyalty of his people and the machinations of his enemies, but he deemed it the best course to take no notice of it; however, he deputed Molwee Hafeezul Islam to Mecca to pray for the prosperity of his affairs.

While a conspiracy was thus formed by the Sindh leader to annihilate the power of the Daoodputra chief, chance brought about an event which entirely occupied Surfaraz Khan at home. About this time, at the instigation of the Raja of Lukhee and Ali Raza, his own father-in-law, he murdered in cold blood Meer Behram Khan of Jalpur while on a visit at his own residence. When the news of this tragedy reached the Subahdar, his son, in a full Durbar, he was naturally much irritated, and forthwith proceeded, full of revenge, to Shedadpur. Surfaraz Khan, anticipating the feelings with which he was actuated, sent a party under the command of Allah Buksh, the son of the Lukhee chief, with directions to destroy him; but he was desperately opposed by the offended Subahdar, and by a single stroke of his sword was laid dead at his feet. The Subahdar defended himself boldly, but was at last overpowered by numbers, and, having received several wounds, was also slain. Meer Fatteh Khan, however, secured the fort of Shedadpur, and was joined by Mehrab Jatwee. The Rajah of Lukhee was soon after also gained over by the Meer, and being thus supported by these two noted chiefs, he attacked the fort of Hyderabad, and captured it without much difficulty, when the whole treasure and jewellery fell into his hands. Surfaraz Khan was captured alive, and thrown into prison; while Mohammed Khan, the son of Gholam Shah, was raised to the vacant Musnud; but was dethroned after six months, and was succeeded by Meean Golam Nabee.

In the meantime Behar Khan, the son of Fatteh Khan, who had gone on a pilgrimage to Mecca, returned from that country, and having landed at Kerachee, which then belonged to Meer Nasir Khan Berohee, took up his quarters in a village named Kharia, in the Jeyselmeer territory. His return was hailed with the greatest joy by Gholam Nabee, who sent several letters advising him to proceed to the capital. His approach, however, was looked upon with the greatest jealousy by Shahbehar and Mehrab Jetawee, who marched out to prevent his arrival, when a dispute occurred, in which Behar proved victorious. The latter appeared much annoyed at the conduct of Gholam Nabee's people, and had him murdered here, with many others of his chief officers. Abdunnabee, the governor of the fort of Hyderabad, on hearing of this atrocious deed, by way of retaliation unmercifully put to the sword Meean Surfaraz Khan, Ater Khan, and Mohammed Khan his son, who were in confinement in the fort.

As Surfaraz Khan was an intelligent and clever man, and had experience enough to be a governor, it was the wish of Behar Khan to restore him to the throne; but Abdunnabee, who himself aspired to that rank, summarily put him out of the way. He was now the only person to whom they could look; and he was therefore, as a matter of necessity, invested with the charge of the government by Behar, while he himself accepted the office of minister under him. This government, however, never regained its former stability.

Meanwhile the province of Multan having been rented to Shareef Khan Suddoozye by Timur Shah, Nawab Shuja Khan, its governor, retired to Shujabad; and having well fortified the place, went alone to Bahawalpur to visit the Khan, where he met with a civil reception. His successor, being a man of indolence and pleasure, the government share of rent soon fell into arrears. This negligence caused the appointment of a collector on the part of his majesty. Mirza Shareef Beg was selected, and deputed on that duty. The Mirza, as was expected, was received coldly by Shareef Khan; which circumstance induced him to go back to court and obtain a lease of the province in his own name, in conjunction with Dharamdas a merchant. This arrangement excluded Shareef from the government of Multan, and obliged him to retire to Bahawalpur. The mutual cordiality, however, between Dahramdas and the Mirza was but of a short duration. A squabble ensued, in which the son-in-law of the former was killed, and he himself plundered of all his property. The Mirza, apprehending a severe retaliation from his majesty's government, tried to secure himself from the impending vengeance. With this view, he invited Gunda Sing and Jhanda Sing, the two Sikh chieftains, who accepted the invitation most cheerfully, and readily proceeded to Multan to aid the Mirza. He afterwards indiscreetly made his escape, first, to the village of Talanba, and afterwards to Kheirpur Tanwein, where he soon after died a natural death.

It has already been stated that the officers of the Khan had entered into a conspiracy against him with Surfaraz Khan, and had thereby offended their chief; the latter, however, delayed showing his serious displeasure. Gholam Hussain meanwhile had put an end to his existence by poison, and the rest had been got rid of, some by voluntary resignation and retirement, and others by suspension from their respective situations. Hence the whole management of affairs devolved on Kader Ali and Behram Ali, the two meritorious officers.

In the year 1191 (A.D. 1777), Nawab Mohammed Muzuffir Khan, the son of Shuja Khan Suddoozye, succeeded his father in the estate of Shujabad. The young chief, however, was often harassed by the incursions of Jhanda Sing and Gunda Sing, the governors of Multan. At last he was obliged to retire to Bahawalpur, when the Khan was moved with compassion at his condition. Thus actuated by friendly feelings, the Daoodputra chief at once proceeded with his own Khans and troops to Multan along with the young chief, and laid siege to that place. The siege was carried on most vigorously, and on the twenty-third day an entrance was forced into the town by means of a widow named Rajoo, when several of the Kaffirs or infidels were slain, and the rest obliged to take shelter in the fort; while the victors gave themselves up to plunder. After having acquired valuable booty, they returned homewards without the permission of their chiefs. Gunda Sing having in the meantime arrived from Lahore with a large force, a severe conflict again ensued, in which the two Mohammedan chiefs were driven back upon Shujabad, and thence, on the third day, Bahawal Khan moved to Bahawalpur.

When the account of this disaster reached the ear of his majesty, he forthwith despatched Sirdar Behrwer Khan with instructions to expel the Sikhs from the Multan territory. The Sirdar, however, owing to the great distance, did not reach his destination before the commencement of the following year. He at once proceeded to lay siege to the fort, and was on the eve of capturing it, when unfortunately he was recalled by the king. The Sirdar, in obedience to the orders of his majesty, immediately raised the siege and returned to the court at Cabul.

He was succeeded in his duty by Sirdar Maded Khan, who had hardly employed himself in the accomplishment of the object of his deputation, when he was also recalled; and, like his predecessor, returned without doing any thing decisive. The king then proceeded in person on the expedition with a large force. After the usual marches, he at length reached the vicinity of Multán, when the royal troops laid siege to the fort. Soon after, the Sikhs, feeling their inability to retain the fort, offered to surrender it, on condition of being allowed to retire unmolested. This request was acceded to. Nawab Muzuffir Khan was invested with the government of Multan, whilst his majesty returned to Cabul.

In the year 1193 Hijra (A. D. 1779), the heir apparent, Mobarik Khan, deputed Kazim Ali Khan to the court of Shah Alum, the Delhi emperor, with a view of obtaining some marks of honour for his master. He was received favourably. After some little time, a Firman, or mandate, was issued in the name of Bahawal Khan, conferring on him the dignity of the Lord of Kehchee, and the Khetab, or title of *Rukduddabh Hafiz-ul-Mulk Nusrat Jung Mohammed Bahawàl Khan Abbasee*, *i. e.* the pillar of the kingdom, the guardian of the country, the victorious in the field, Mohammed Bahawal Khan Abbasee. The Vakeel shortly after returned, and waited on his master, with the Firman and Khelat, or dress of honor, as is customary on such occasions. Bahawal Khan was of course highly gratified at these royal distinctions. About this time, Abdul Kareem Khan Baber, one of the chief officers of Muzuffir Khan, by the permission of his master, attacked and plundered a village belonging to Bahawalpur, situated on the Multan side of the river. The Khan was very much offended at this unprovoked aggression; and, in order to revenge himself, instantly despatched his troops to the spot. A battle followed between the two parties, when Abdul Kareem, together with some other officers of note, was killed; and his men repulsed with some loss, both in killed and wounded.

In this year 1194 Hijra (1780, A. D.), the Khan obtained the lease of the Pergunnah of Jetwal and Medwola, from the Nazim of the Dereh of Ghazi Khan. A matrimonial connection was also made about this time between the daughter of Mohammed Khan Berjanee, and Bahawal Khan.

The changes which had been brought about by Meer Bahar Khan, in the government of Sindh, had been entirely disapproved of by the Khorasan monarch, and Bujjee Sing, the chief of Jodhpur, as well as by the other chiefs of the neighbourhood. Besides this, the mother of Abdunnabee had originally been displeased with him, for the murder of her elder son, but waited for a favourable time to take revenge upon him. The disposition evinced by the neighbouring chiefs, gave her the opportunity which she had so long sought for. She was, moreover, encouraged in her design, by Sheikh Mehfooz, and two or three other officers; and was induced to communicate her grievances to the

Jodhpur chief, and to solicit his aid in getting rid of Behar. The Raja, whose mind was already poisoned against the Meer, undertook, without hesitation, to favor her cause. With this view, he engaged two Rajputs, on promise of granting them an annual Jaghir of 30,000 rupees, in the Nagur province, to assassinate Behar; and these ruffians soon after proceeded to the court of the Sindh chief, under the disguise of agents. On their arrival, they were admitted by Behar to a private interview, when, in the course of conference, they at once seized the Meer, and mortally wounded him in the belly with a knife, of which wound he instantly died.

When this murder was committed, Fatteh Khan, and Abdullah, the sons of the late Behar, were at Shadadpur. As soon as they heard of the perfidious assassination of their father, they declared Meean Sadik Khan, one of the descendants of Deen Mohammed Khaloora, the ruler of the country. This proceeding occasioned a great revolution in the land, and obliged Gholam Nabee to fly to Khelat, and to sue for the assistance of Nasir Khan Berohee, in maintaining him in the government of Sindh. He also sent his sons with the same view to the Raja of Jodhpur; but the latter, owing to the cordial relationship which already existed between the two parties, immediately despatched a large force along with the young chief On their reaching Sindh, they forced the usurper to a pitched battle; but were at last discomfited with great loss, and driven from the field. As soon as the accounts of this defeat had reached Abdunnabee, he proceeded in person to the scene of action, with Nasir

Khan, and his troops; but, on his being opposed by Sadik, he met with the same fate as his sons.

Nasir Khan being now no longer able to support the cause of his guest, made some provisions for his expenses, by assigning to him one-half of the revenue of Hajjipur, in the district of the Dereh of Ghazi Khan. He accordingly sent him to take charge of the assignment; but no sooner had he secured this possession, than he went off to the court of Timur Shah to solicit his majesty's aid in restoring him to his country. His request was favourably received, and Maded Khan was accordingly despatched with a detachment of royal troops, to see his restoration effected. On his arrival in Sindh, a prolonged discussion ensued between the two parties. At last, it was arranged, that Abdul Nabee should ascend the throne of Sindh, while Abdullah, the son of Bahar, was to accept the office of Vizir under him.

On the 15th of Safer, 1195 (A. D. 1780), Bahawal Khan was favoured by the birth of another son, who was named Abdullah, well-known by the name of Mohammed Sadik Khan.

The same year is also remarkable for the death of the Mukdoom Sahib of Uch. He was succeeded by his eldest son, Mohammed Ghoree, who did not survive his father long, but soon followed him to Paradise. His younger brother, whose revolt will be described in its proper place, succeeded him.

Maded Khan, who had arrived in Sindh on the part of Timur Shah, now returned to the court. But the arrangements which had been patched up by him, regarding the new administration, were dissolved on his departure. Abdunnabee, who all along entertained strong suspicions of the fidelity of his Vizir Abdullah, and Fatteh Khan his brother, had them apprehended and murdered. Fatteh Ali Khan, the son of the late Subahdar, and Meir Sahib, etc., considering their continuance in the country rather unsafe, retired to the Gurhee Ikhtyar Khan; but not being favourably received, they went on to Fazul Ali Khan Halanee, and took up their quarters in Deenghur. After the assassination of the late Vizir, a person of the Jatwee tribe, named Dhakana, rose into favour in the court of Abdunnabee. He was at once raised to a high rank by the gift of the insignia of the Nakara and Neshan, or a kettle drum and a flag, as well as by the grant of a Jaghir of 3,000 or 4,000 rupees; and he was, besides this, distinguished by being invested with the command of troops.

While these arrangements were going on in court, Sohrab and Fatteh Ali were not idle in their retreat. They employed themselves actively in collecting as many troops as their means would admit, chiefly from the Khosa tribe. When they had completed their equipment, they moved to the village of Abawrasa. On hearing of their hostile movements, Abdunnabee sent out his new favourite at the head of his own troops to oppose the invaders; but the young commander had not the same experience as his antagonists in the field; and, consequently, on his approach, he was surprised by a night attack, in which he was defeated, and put to flight, leaving the whole encampment, baggage and all, in the hands of the Meers. The victors, flushed with success, advanced with slow but steady movements. Abdunnabee despatched another detachment under the command of Hussain Ali, also newly raised; but, on coming into contest with the enemy, he met with the same reverse as his predecessor, with the difference only that he was himself killed in the battle. In short, the last discomfiture alarmed the chief so much, that, entertaining fears for his own safety, he hurriedly made his escape to the court of Khorasan, even leaving his family behind at Hyderabad. Meean Sadik Khaloora was considered unworthy of the throne. The nomination of Meer Fatteh Ali was in consequence secured by a great outlay of money, in the Durranee court, while Abdunnabee, having obtained a lease of Dereh Ghazi Khan for a lakh of rupees, arrived at Hajjipur. The new chief, in order to conciliate his colleague, Sohrab, conferred on him one-third of the Sindh territory, and one-tenth was at the same time given to Meer Tahara.

In the beginning of A.D. 1198 the fort of Hyderabad was also captured. Every respect was, however, shown to the females of the ex-chief who had been left behind, and they were honourably removed to Hajjipur to join Abdunnabee. Among them were the Maee Khanum Begum, the daughter of the late Jaunesar and widow of Gholam Shah; and Sone Baee, the daughter of Norung Khan Billotch and widow of Surfaraz. They proceeded to Bahawalpur, and staid with Allahdad Khan, the son of Jaunesar. Being of the Abbasee tribe, they were treated with marked consideration and hospitality by the Khan.

Since 1197 Hijra (A.D. 1782), Hajee Ikhtyar and Fazul Khan, the two nobles of Bahawal Khan's court, had appeared somewhat disaffected towards their master.

They were now brought back to their senses by the infliction of proper punishment.

Ahmed Khan Peerjanee, the founder of the town of Ahmedpur, died about this time. Owing to a quarrel among his heirs, his youngest son, Mohebbat, took shelter with the Khan; and soon after gave the hand of his daughter in marriage to Bahawal Khan, at the same time conferring on the latter in dowry the town of Ahmedpur as well as the canal of Kutubwah.

Although Abdunnabee retired from the active scenes of public life, he still had not banished from his mind the idea of being once more restored to the throne of Sindh; and with this view he maintained a constant correspondence with the court of Timur Shah. His object, however, did not long remain concealed from Fatteh Ali Khan, the present chief, who, in order to thwart it, deputed, on his own part, a Persian named Ibrahim, who was well versed in the politics of the times, to wait on his majesty. On his arrival at the court, he interested, by his adroitness and conciliating manners, almost all the courtiers in behalf of his master. This favourable change induced the latter to make his appearance before his majesty, and endeavour to be formally recognised as the ruler of Sindh. The king, however, declared that whoever would pay him first, in ready cash, nine lakhs of rupees within six days, should be acknowledged the sovereign of the country. Abdunnabee was unable to meet the royal demand, which was readily satisfied by his rival Fatteh Ali. He was accordingly favoured with a Khelat, and a deed of grant of Sindh; and thus acknowledged by royalty, he returned to his country.

The internal management of the civil and financial affairs of the territory of Sindh had for a long time past been in charge of Dewan Guddoomul. Every one who gratified the cupidity of that functionary was allowed to continue unmolested; but those who were in the least opposed to him, were sure to meet with ruin. The present chief was not uninformed of the roguery of his minister, but waited for an opportunity to punish him. Being now secured in his possessions by the royal order, he had nothing further to fear from his officers; and accordingly his first act on his return was to seize the Dewan, and to deprive him of his whole property and treasure, which was immense; but as he did not consider this disgrace enough, the Dewan and his brother were soon after put to death by his order, while the females of his family were compelled to embrace the religion of Mohammed.

In the very same year, Bahawal Khan succeeded in digging two wells of sweet water in the woods; and also rebuilt the fort of Vinjrot, which had been in a state of ruin for many years. Another fort, called Khangur, was likewise built in the same wood, about 20 koss to the south of Deirawer.

The Jamahmasjid (mosque) of Ahmedpur, a handsome and pretty building, was also built by the Khan in the year 1199 Hijra (A.D. 1784).

Hajji Ikhtyar Khan, who had been ill-disposed towards Bahawal Khan, had lately been on a pilgrimage to Mecca; but his visit to that holy temple had made no change in his enmity towards the Khan. He entered into a contest about the boundary of Ilahabad; but not being able to resist the troops, which were led against him by the Khan in person, he shut himself up in his own Gurhee, where he was besieged; but was subsequently pardoned through the intercession of Mukdoom Gunj Buksh.

Intelligence was received of the natural death of Guj Sing, the chief of Bikaner; and he was succeeded by his son Rae Sing, who had only reigned fourteen days, when he was poisoned by his own servants, and his youngest son was raised to the vacated Musnud, while Surat Sing, his uncle, was selected to act as his Vizir. The latter, however, to pave a way for his own succession, terminated the life of his young nephew by poison; and also caused several of the chief officers from whom he apprehended the least resistance, to be unmercifully murdered.

The ill success which Abdunnabee had lately experienced in the Khorasan court had not driven him to despair. He still carried on his designs in the court; and in the furtherance of them, he sent a man named Kumruddeen, who tried to impress on his majesty's mind, that, owing to the enmity of his master, a combination had been made between all the Sindh chiefs and Fatteh Ali, and also between the latter and Bahawal Khan. This, as well as other selfish misrepresentations, roused political suspicions in the mind of the Shah, who forthwith issued a violent note in his own handwriting to the Daoodputra chief. The following is the translation of it:—

"Shahnawaz Khan Bahadar Abbassee is sent by me, at the head of a detachment of royal troops, with other officers of high rank, to conquer the territory of Sindh.

I am extremely displeased with you for having repeatedly supported the Faulpur people and sheltered them in your own forts, and permitted the Daoodputras to assist them. And I hereby intimate, that if in future you exert yourself in aiding Shahnawaz in extirpating that people, well and good; but if you act otherwise, you will be among the first to receive due punishment from my hands."

"Dated 9th Teirmah Ilahee, year 12."

About this time, Sheikh Mukdoom Geelanee died, and was succeeded by his younger son, Mohammed Ghaus, who assumed the title of Hamed Gunj Buksh. A detailed account of him will appear hereafter.

In the same year, Said Hajji Shah, a dependant of the Marufanee house, came over to Bahawal Khan, by whom he was taken into favour, and raised to the rank of Vizir.

It has been already stated, that the king was preparing an expedition to Sindh under the superintendence of Shahnawaz; but the management appears to have been transferred to Sirdar Maded-Khan Durranee, although the reason of it is uncertain.

In 1200 Hijra (A.D. 1785), this officer set out with the royal troops to conquer Sindh for Abdunnabee; but, first he directed his movements towards Bahawalpur. On the road, he was joined by his ally; and on his approach to Khanghur, by Muzuffir-Khan, the governor of Multan, who was received in a very friendly manner. Bahawal Khan, on hearing of the Sirdar's advance towards his own territory, betook himself to the fort of Deirawer; while Kareem Khan, and other Daoodputra chiefs of the Arbanee and Ghumranee tribes, secured the two forts situated in the Cholistan. The Khan was also soon after joined by Jalal Khan and Fazul Ali, the chiefs of the Holanee tribe, together with other Khans, as well as Mukdoom Hamed of Uch, with his family. A newswriter on the part of the Khan was already present in the camp of Maded Khan. He now deputed two other persons, named Mohammed Beg and Jeewan Ram, to wait on the Sirdar. On their arrival they were admitted to an audience, when they delivered the messages with which they had been charged by their master. Meanwhile he was joined by Noor Mohammed, the head of the Marufanee tribe, as well as by Khoda Buksh and Ameer Khan of Kheirpur, and the chief of the Telhanee tribe, besides several other Daoodputra chiefs who had been ill-disposed towards Bahawal Khan. They made every representation which might inflame the fury of the Sirdar against the latter. Thus instigated by them, as well as by Abdunnabee, the Sirdar at once advanced on Bahawalpur; and on crossing the river, he put the agents of the Khan in confinement. On his entering into Bahawalpur, he ordered the palace and the mirror-room of the Khan, and also the houses of his nobles, to be set on fire, and thus reduced them to ashes; while the troops were permitted to carry out their depredations as far as Kheirpur and Kaempur, and to demolish every stone building within their reach, besides the Khan's own house, which was situated at Ahmedpur.

After the Durranee chief had indulged his revenge thus far, he forwarded the Rakum, or mandate, of the Shah, together with his own letter to Bahawal Khan, by the hand of Sohrab Beg, a Kuzilbash, and Ostakahee, a blacksmith, demanding him to depute his son to join him in capturing Sindh for Abdunnabee, in order to please his majesty. Accordingly, the Khan deputed his eldest son, Mobarik, to wait on the Sirdar, and at the same time personally inspected his troops in the presence of Maded's agents, who expressed their wonder at observing their good discipline. The agents, accompanied by the young Khan, were dismissed with Khelats. On his arrival, Mobarik was received with proper consideration by Maded Khan; and much friendly conversation passed between them.

In his progress towards Bahawalpur, the Sirdar had laid siege to the fortress of Peer Saadet, belonging to the Daoodputras; but in his hurry to reach Bahawalpur, he had raised the siege without accomplishing his object; and thereby, as he stated, had sustained some loss; in compensation for which, he demanded the payment of a sum of 6,000 rupees, which was readily agreed to by the young Khan.

Notwithstanding his giving such satisfaction, Maded made two attempts to take the fort of Deirawer, belonging to Bahawal Khan. The Khan was consequently obliged to send out a force under the command of Fazul Ali, to oppose him. He fought very bravely, and killed numbers of the enemy. This reverse induced the Sirdar to advance in person against the fort, and to occupy an advantageous position at Murrava, between Ahmedpur and Deirawer. Some overtures were at first exchanged; but, eventually, it was arranged, that the Khan should pay a sum of 60,000 rupees as Nuzrana, to pacify the exasperated enemy. In accordance with this arrangement, the father of the chief, Fatteh Khan, waited on Maded in his camp, and paid him the stipulated amount.

On the payment of the Nuzrana, the royal troops bent their course towards Sindh, and quitted the Bahawalpur territory; upon which the peasantry, and other people, who had deserted the country to escape the fury of the enemy, returned to their habitations. The Khan also returned to Bahawalpur.

Khummon Khan, a Mallah, or boatman, who had distinguished himself by his valorous conduct during the late disaster, in suppressing the predatory incursions of the Khans of the Marufanee tribe, who infested the country, was raised to the high rank of governor of the fort of Khanghur.

The royal troops, on their arrival, made a halt near Kheirpur Taranda, and thence a deputation was despatched to Meer Sohrab, the chief of Kheirpur, to ask his aid in the restoration of Abdunnabee to Sindh. This deputation consisted of Taj Mohammed, the son of Abdunnabee, with four other Motbers, or confidential men, on the part of the latter, and Sohrab Beg on that of Maded Khan. The Meer, however, refused to comply with their request; and the deputation in consequence returned without effecting its object. The Sirdar was of course displeased at the failure of his mission, and now exerted himself in collecting as many more mercenaries as he could from the neighbourhood. With these raw levies, in conjunction with the royal troops, he renewed his march on Hyderabad; and, on his arrival within two koss of that place, he took up his quarters at Khodabad, from whence he addressed a letter to Fatteh Ali, calling upon him, as he had been desired by the Shah, to restore the Sindh territory to Abdunnabee, and threatening, that, in the event of his refusing, he would be visited with the royal displeasure.

Fatteh Ali, as was expected, refused to obey the order without trying the issue of a contest in the field. With this view, he removed his property and family to Kuch Bujh, and he himself set about collecting his scattered troops, and making other warlike preparations. At length, he encountered his antagonist in the field, when a severe action was fought, in which he was eventually overcome, and repulsed, with great loss. He made his escape towards Kuch Bujh, to join his family.

Abdunnabee was now reinstalled, and restored to his territory, when Maded, as the object of his expedition had been fully attained, returned to Cabul.

It appears that Abdunnabee was not a popular ruler, and was generally disliked, while a favourable disposition still prevailed towards Fatteh Ali. Notwithstanding his energetic efforts, he did not succeed in reconciling the people, and restoring tranquillity to the country. At last, finding his position unsafe among a disaffected people, he again retired to Hajjipur without fighting, and reported his proceeding to Timur Shah, who was extremely exasperated at the continued disobedience of Fatteh Ali.

In the ensuing cold weather, his majesty proceeded in person on the second expedition against Sindh, by way of the Derehjats. On his approach to Khanghur in the Multan province, he was waited upon by the governor. The Khan, apprehending further misfortunes, removed his Harems first to the fort of Sirdarghur, and thence to Wunjrut and Hasilpur, while he himself entrusted the custody of the fort of Deirawer to Alum Khan of the Beloochee tribe, and took up his abode in the Bikaner and Jeyselmeer territories, where he amused himself chiefly in shooting excursions. In the meantime, the Khans of the Marufanee and Mundhanee tribes waited on the Shah, and as they had been originally impressed with bad designs, they now renewed their slanders against the Khan. The royal camp accordingly moved to Bahawalpur, and the country was again subjected to the plunder and devastations of the unruly troops, while Maded Khan was despatched to reduce the fort of Deirawer. As he was provided with besieging engines, the garrison was soon compelled to sue for peace, and the keys were immediately made over by Alum Khan to the Sirdar; upon which he himself was allowed to pass out unmolested. He next deputed an agent, named Izzet Rae, to the Shah, to appease the royal displeasure. The agent was admitted to an audience through the interest of Noor Mohammed Khan Baber, the Ameen-ul-Mulk, who was a friend of the Khan, and was favourably received.

As soon as Bahawal Khan's arrival in the Marwar territory was brought under the notice of Surat Sing, the chief of the country, he took measures to treat him very hospitably, and also opened a friendly correspondence with him. The Khan, however, being very cautious, did not stay in one place, but moved about to elude any machinations of his enemies.

Notwithstanding this, the Shah, having heard a good deal of his high qualifications, both public and private, was now favourably disposed, and, through the Ameen-ul-Mulk, Maded, and Abdunnabee, expressed his wish, that if the Khan would send his son to wait on his majesty with proper tribute and presents, he would be favourably received. No sooner was the royal wish communicated by his agents, than the Khan deputed his son, Mobarik, along with three Motbers, with the demanded Nuzrana to the Shah. Through the medium of Ameen-ul-Mulk, they were admitted to the royal presence, and were kindly received. The young Khan was invested with a Khelat, together with a Chogha, or embroidered cloak, besides a Rakum, securing the restoration of territory in the name of the Khan himself. An annual assignment of 12,000 rupees from the revenue of Multan was also made in favour of Mobarik. Thus favoured, the latter was dismissed, to return and to report the result to his father.

The lease of Multan was at the same time renewed in favour of Muzuffir Khan, and the conduct of the affairs of the Dereh of Ghazi Khan, with its dependencies, as well as the custody of the fort of Deirawer, was made over to the charge of Shah Mohammed Khan, an Afghan of the Baduzaee tribe, and a native of Multan. The fort was accordingly garrisoned by Afghans of his party, who seized and imprisoned some of the Daoodputra Khans; while the possessions of the Khan situated on the right bank of the river in the Dereh province, were rented by his majesty to a Goojer named Moladad.

While the king was engaged in making these arrangements, his attention was drawn to a sudden insurrection in Turan, which expedited his return to Cabul, with a view of proceeding to Balkh to quell the rebellion, without accomplishing the object of his expedition, making, however, some provision for Abdunnabee by granting him an assignment of 40,000 rupees from Multan.

On this occasion, the Shah admitted into his Harem the daughter of Fatteh Khan, who was allied by matrimonial connection to Peer Mohammed, as well as the daughter of Heyat Khan Khaloora, the chief of Sindh.

On being apprised of Timur Shah's hasty return towards Balkh, Bahawal Khan returned to Bahawalpur, and soon after moved to Uch, in order to contrive the recovery of the fort of Deirawer. The families of the Afghans who occupied that fort were secured in the fort of Seitpur on the right bank of the Sutlej. With the view of attacking that place and of seizing them, he collected about three hundred boats at the ferry of Uch; and having crossed the river by this means, he surprised the place, and easily got possession of the inmates. They were removed very disgracefully, and exposed before the fort of Deirawer. The Afghans, in order to secure their Nung or reputation, could not do otherwise than surrender the fort on condition of obtaining the liberation of their families. They were allowed to pass with them unmolested to Dereh-deen-panah in the province of Dereh Ghazi Khan; while the Khan, by this contrivance, peaceably recovered the best fort of his whole territory.

Mohammed Beg and Chein Rae were taken into confidence and entrusted with the signet of the Khan, while Behar Rae, a Gosaeen, was admitted into his councils in civil matters.

Notwithstanding his repeated failures, Meean Abdunnabee continued from time to time to urge his restoration to Sindh on the attention of the Shah. A third expedition was, therefore, now organised in his behalf, and conducted by Paenda Khan, an Afghan of the Barakzaee tribe. In the beginning of the cold weather, he arrived at Dereh Ghazi Khan, where he was joined by the Meean; and crossing the Indus below Mithankot, advanced on Sindh. On his arrival at Shikarpur he was joined by Nasir Khan Berohee with a considerable force. In the meantime, Fatteh Ali, who had again occupied the territory on the retreat of Abdunnabee, on being informed of Paenda Khan's advance, had deputed agents to the court to try and secure his own position and stability by being recognised by his majesty. By expending a large sum, the agents succeeded, through Kazee Feizullah, in restoring the goodwill of the Shah towards their master, and Fatteh Ali was accordingly confirmed in his possession, and a royal mandate issued to Paenda Khan on the receipt of the usual Nuzrana to acknowledge his authority, and then to return to court. In obedience to his instructions, the Sirdar, in consequence, soon after moved out to Candahar by way of Khelat; while Abdunnabee, being again disappointed, retired to his asylum at Hajjipur.

Aref Khan, his son, who had been deputed to Jodhpur to procure some aid from the chief of that state, to enable his father to prosecute his designs against Sindh with better means, also failed in his object. As soon as he heard of his father's retreat, he left that court and retraced his steps to join his father. On his way thither he met Bahawal Khan at Deirawer, where he was received with the usual hospitality. The Khan moreover paid him a visit in his own tent, to console him for the misfortunes of his family.

Aref continued in this place for a few days, and on his departure was presented with some valuable articles. He crossed the river at Uch, and soon reached Hajjipur, where he reported the result of his mission to his father.

Thus seeing himself deprived of all support in every quarter, Abdunnabee once more brought forward his claims in the Khorasan court. Since misfortunes always attract compassion, the Shah was naturally much moved at his deplorable condition; and in consequence authorised him to occupy the province of Bhakar and Leiya, which were in the possession of the Beloochees. He also assured him, that, in the accomplishment of this object, he was to be assisted by the governor of Multan, as well as by several Jaghirdars of that quarter. Orders were at the same time issued by the king to the above authorities and to the managers of Derehjats on the subject. Muzuffir Khan, however, avoided assisting him; but he was supported by others, in accordance with the instructions of his majesty. Accompanied by these allies, he crossed the Indus near Sungar, and soon came in contact with the Beloochees. Heyat, their chief, had just died, and had been succeeded by his brother, Mohammed Khan, who marched out to oppose Abdunnabee in the field; but after a severe struggle, was repulsed and compelled to throw himself into a fort named Munkeira, while the fortress of Noushehra was secured by his servant Lukman. The latter, however, soon fell into the hands of the enemy, who soon afterwards reduced the whole province, except the fort of Munkeira, which remained unsubdued.

After Abdunnabee had established his authority throughout the country, he advanced upon this place also; but, owing to its great strength, his attempt was thwarted. In this emergency, he applied to the king for reinforcement, and strict orders were issued in consequence by express to Muzuffir Khan, to give the aid solicited by him. The Multan governor accordingly joined him in a short time. His mere arrival was sufficient to spread a panic among the garrison; and, Mohammed, fearing lest he should fall prisoner into the hands of the enemy, made his escape. The evacuated fort was then occupied by Abdunnabee without further resistance. He now proceeded peaceably to devote his attention to the internal management of his newly acquired possessions.

It is already known that Khoda Buksh, Khodayar, and Talib Khan, etc., etc., the chiefs of the Marufanee tribe, were very much opposed to the Khan. Failing to secure assistance in other quarters, they had recourse to the court of Bikaner, where they had easy access to Surat Singh, the chief, through one of his servants Sawaee Shah. They applied to him for aid to enable them to reduce the fortress of Majghur, in the Bahawalpur territory. In compliance with their entreaties, the chief placed at their disposal a party of his troops under the command of one of his own officers, Sada Golab. The Marufanee chiefs, having united their own troops with those of the Rajah, proceeded without delay to Majghur, and succeeded in reducing it by siege, without meeting with much resistance. On being apprised of the rapid progress of the insurgents, the Khan sent his own force, under the command of Alum Khan, to punish them. The opposing armies came into collision near Kheirpur, and a bloody fight ensued; but, at last the insurgents, feeling their inability to continue the contest, took to flight towards Cholistan. Alum Khan was liberally rewarded for his brave conduct in suppressing the rebellion.

A misunderstanding appears to have taken place between the Khan and his son Mobarik about this time. It appears that the former ordered a Jaghir of 12,000 rupees to be conferrred on the son of the latter; but owing to some negligence on the part of the officers employed, a delay occurred in the execution of the orders. This circumstance annoyed Mobarik; and in the impulse of the moment, he observed, that when he should reign after the death of his father, he would punish the officers with dismissal and disgrace. This remark was attributed to his disrespect towards his father; and he was accordingly prohibited from visiting the court in future.

On being firmly established in the province of Bhakar and Leiya, Abdunnabee, instigated by Mohammed Hamed, Geelanee, frequently interfered with the affairs of Bahawalpur. This interference, however, was not of long duration; for the lease of the province having been granted to Kumr-ud-Deen by the Shah, he was obliged to proceed again to his majesty's court, where, after some time, he succeeded in obtaining its restoration.

Timur Shah was, at this time, struck with a paralytic stroke which soon terminated his life. His death appears to have given rise to no disturbance at the time; for Prince Zaman, who was then the governor of Cabul, was unanimously declared his successor by his chief officers, such as Rahmutullah Khan Suddoozye, and Paenda Khan, and Barakzaee, etc., etc. He was immediately placed on the vacant throne and each person tendered his allegiance without resistance.

To reward the loyalty of Rahmutullah, the new king raised him to the high office of Vizir, distinguishing him by the title of Wafadar Khan, while Paendeh Khan was honoured with the title of Surfaraz Khan. The other officers and functionaries of the court were likewise distinguished by the bestowal of Khelats and promotion according to their respective grades.

In the same year, the king proceeded on a journey to Peshawur and the Derehjats, to receive the homage of his subjects in that quarter. Bahawal Khan deputed his son Feizullah Khan to wait on his majesty, to condole with him on the death of the late monarch, and to congratulate the present king on his succession. Muzuffir Khan also proceeded to the royal camp for the same purpose; and both of them were received and dismissed with proper honours.

Among others, Abdunnabee waited on his majesty at the same time. As there was a government claim against him for 120,000 rupees, on account of arrears of revenue, he was called upon to pay it; but, through the interposition of Muzuffir Khan, the presentation of five hundred camels was agreed to in lieu of that sum. As he was unable readily to fulfil even that part of the stipulation, he was obliged to leave his grandson Gholam

Ali, then ten years old, as a hostage in the royal camp, until the claim was satisfied. After this the king returned to Cabul.

Abdunnabee was still unable to produce the stipulated number of camels; and his young grandson was advised by his guardian (a Hindu), to get admission into the Harem of the Vizir. Here he began to weep so, that his lamentations moved the wife of the minister with compassion; she interfered with her husband to have the royal claim remitted, and he was accordingly dismissed to his family. Abdunnabee naturally expressed his most grateful thanks to the court for its unexpected liberality.

In this year, the marriage of Abdullah, the youngest son of the Khan, was celebrated with the grand-daughter of Ali Morad Khan.

About the same period, Nawab Zulfikar Khan, one of the nobles of high rank of Madhojee Sindhia's court passed by Bahawalpur to Cabul, accompanied by Gholam Mohammed Populzae who had been deputed by the Durranee monarch to Sindhia. Besides many valuable presents, he had charge of three elephants for the Khorasan monarch. The deputation was treated with marked hospitality by the Khan on its arrival at Bahawalpur.

Prince Humayun, being the eldest son of Timur Shah, was, of course, much annoyed at the proclamation of Zaman Shah, as king; and to support his claim of priority, he soon set about collecting as many troops as he could in Candahar, where he took up his residence on the death of his father. The king, on being apprised of his brother's mischievous design, lost no time in proceeding personally to that quarter to suppress the insurrection. On his approach to Candahar, he addressed a letter to Humayun, inviting him to wait on his majesty, when he would be received with proper consideration; and threatening him with punishment in case of disobedience. The prince, convinced of his right of birth, and at the same time instigated by self-interested counsellors, who are never wanting on such occasions, refused to comply with his majesty's request, and forthwith marched out with his troops to oppose the royal army. A severe contest ensued, when the prince, having been totally defeated, fled, and betook himself to a wandering life.

Notwithstanding the indulgence shewn to Abdunnabee in the remission of the royal claim, he still failed to pay the further government dues. Besides this, many complaints of his oppression of the Ryots were repeatedly received against him in the court. Before the king departed on his expedition to Candahar, he had summoned him to join his majesty with all his available troops, but he still avoided obedience to the royal mandate. This so exasperated his majesty, that Abdunnabee was ordered to be dismissed and to be expelled from the Leiya province, while Mohammed Khan, otherwise called Nawab Surfaraz Khan, was nominated his successor. Instructions were, at the same time, issued to the governors of Multan and the Derehjats, to assist him in recovering the province from the present possessor. The new governor, accordingly, soon made his appearance in the vicinity of Leiya, where he was opposed by Abdunnabee. A skirmish ensued, in which his son Aref, as well as Abdurraheem Baber, and Surfaraz Khan Baduzaee, were slain. The fall of these chieftains so dispirited Abdunnabee, that he sued for peace, which was granted. The keys of the forts were surrendered to the conqueror, and the expelled governor was allowed to quit the province with his family unmolested. For a few days he staid in a village called Peipla, opposite to Uch; and afterwards proceeded to Jeyselmeer, whence he proceeded to the court of the Jodhpur chief, Bheim Sing, the grandson of Bujjee Sing, his old friend, who received him kindly, and made suitable provision for his expenses, giving him two villages for that purpose. Mohammed Khan, his successor, took every pains to restore order in the country. The Ryots soon began to have confidence in him; and trade revived.

On the flight of Humayun, orders were issued to all the governors of the realm to seize the prince, whenever and wherever he might be found. A short time after, he came down by the pass of Bora to Leiya, with his family and servants, and stopped for some little time at a well in the vicinity of that place. No sooner was this intelligence brought to the governor, than he forthwith proceeded to the place to seize the fugitive prince, who had no time to effect his escape, and therefore prepared himself for opposition. As the governor approached, his servants fired a volley at the prince, which killed two or three of his party. The fire was returned with greater effect; for Sultan the son of the Shahzada and a nephew of Vizir Fatteh Khan, together with some others, were killed. The prince, however, being overpowered by numbers, was taken prisoner along with his Harem and confined in the fort of Bhakar, while the matter was reported to the king; and Mohammed Khan for his valuable services received Khelats and a Rakum of the governorship of Dereh Ismael Khan; and the prince was then cruelly deprived of his sight, and removed with his family to Cabul, where he died soon afterwards.

In this year Sultan Sing, the son of the late Guj Sing, the ruler of Bikaner, who, on the accession of his elder brother Surat Sing, had led a wandering life, arrived at Bahawalpur, and was introduced to the Khan by Beharjee, his chief officer. He was treated with kindness, and on taking leave was presented with suitable gifts.

In the same year, the Khan contracted another marriage with the daughter of Jaun Khan Daoodputra, the lord of Milsean. Gholam Mohammed Khan, the elder brother of Ahmed Ali Khan, the ruler of Rampur, in Rohilkund, offended by the accession of his younger brother and instigated by the Lucknow chief, arrived on his way to Cabul at Bahawalpur, where he was received and treated with proper hospitality. A friendly alliance was thus established between these two persons; and Gholam Mohammed proceeded to his destination by way of Multan and Peshawur; whence, after three months, he returned to India by Bahawalpur. In the same year, an agent of Asfuddola, the ruler of Lucknow, arrived here to induce the Khorasan monarch to undertake an expedition against Hindustan.* During his stay, he was also

* It is not impossible, although hitherto unknown, that some intrigue may have been carried on between the courts of Lucknow and Cabul, encouraging Zaman Shah to undertake his threatened invasion of Hindustan. If this was known to Lord Wellesley, it would be a full justification of his mutilation of the Oude territory.—Ed.

treated with the usual hospitality; and on his departure was presented with the rarities of the country. From Dereh Ismael Khan and Peshawur, the agent despatched a messenger to wait on Zaman Shah with some presents, and to make certain overtures with which he was entrusted. The Durranee monarch, who had already resolved to undertake an expedition to India allured by the representations of Gholam Mohammed, determined at once to carry that resolution into effect, immediately on the appearance of the embassy of the Lucknow ruler. After consulting with his chief officers, the king marched out with a large army towards Lahore, but had hardly proceeded as far as Hussanabdal, when his attention was drawn to an insurrection raised by his step-brother, Mohammed, at Herat, which compelled him to give up the expedition and to turn his arms against his own rival.

A misunderstanding had lately arisen between Mukdoom Hamed of Uch, and the Khan. Being instigated by Mohammed Nobahar of the second Uch, notwithstanding the urgent dissuasions of his own adherents, such as Mehr Shah, Bhaker Shah, Molwee Shah, Mohammed Moladad Khan, and Amer Khan, etc., Hamed continued to evince his ill-will. The persons above named were suspected of being in secret favourably disposed to the Khan, and were therefore falsely accused of having stolen a very valuable jewelled sword and conveyed it to him. On being informed of this groundless charge, Bahawal Khan sent Hamed one of his best swords by his son Sadik Mohammed; but the latter was treated very disrespectfully by the servants of the provoked Hamed, who was not contented with the use of abusive language, but opened a fire on the party of the young Khan, who, however, was unhurt, and reached his father in safety.

Bahawal Khan was naturally exasperated at this insult. The suspicions of the Mukdoom Sahib still continuing against his servants, they were discharged soon afterwards. They immediately proceeded to Bahawalpur and entered the service of the Khan, to whom they obtained ready access by offering him information relative to their late master.

The Khan, being still anxious to pacify Hamed, from motives of respect deputed to him Alum Khan, one of his confidential adherents, with overtures of friendship. As soon as he appeared before him, he was attacked with a volley of abuses, and narrowly escaped with his life.

In consequence of these proceedings, the Khan considered Hamed to have lost his senses; and with this impression, he contrived, in concert with his relations, to have him confined within the walls of his house, and guards placed around to prevent his going out. When the Mukdoom heard of this resolution, he made his escape from Uch along with a party of Sawars, and took up his quarters in the Gurhee or fort of Ikhtyar Khan. Three months afterwards, a reconciliation was brought about between the two parties through the interposition of the son of Ikhtyar Khan; and Hamed accordingly returned to Uch.

This patched-up reconciliation was not of long duration. The Mukdoom's mind was still ill-disposed towards the Khan; and he employed agents with the governors of

Multan and the Bikaner chiefs, as well as in the court of Zaman Shah, to assist him in indulging in his revengeful design. He, however, failed in the two first-named quarters; but an order was received from the king, demanding an explanation of the case. His majesty was, in reply, informed of the insanity of the Mukdoom; while the latter was secured within his house, and guards placed over him to prevent his going out.

He nevertheless effected his escape, and took refuge in a fortress named Ramkolee, situated three koss to the west of Uch. Here he ordered his Sawars to plunder and infest the Ahmedpur roads, which in consequence became very unsafe. He moreover employed some men to murder Sultan, a servant of the Khan, against whom he was also much incensed. The ruffians, however, mistook a Hindu for their victim, and murdered him without scruple under the very walls of Ahmedpur.

The unsafe condition of the road, which was increasing daily, attracted the notice of the Khan, who soon took vigorous measures to put a stop to it; and his displeasure against the offender was much aggravated in consequence.

About this period, Alum Khan, being disaffected towards the Khan, retired with his family to the Gurhee of Ikhtyar Khan; but death soon put a stop to his ill-will. His son, Nasir Khan, who returned to Bahawalpur, was forgiven and again taken into favour.

Khoda Buksh Khan Marufanee, moved by his old enmity, renewed his application to the chief of Bikaner for aid. Surat Sing, perhaps regretting the failure of the late expedition, gave a ready ear to his solicitation, and a detachment was immediately sent under the command of Swaee Shah, the chief commander of his troops. Khoda Buksh, being joined by this party, at once proceeded to Lal Sohara, about twelve koss to the east of Bahawalpur. On hearing of his hostile movements, Bahawal Khan also sent a large force from Deirawer to check his progress; and the two armies came in contact near Sohara. A severe contest ensued; and the rebel, being unable long to withstand the valorous troops of the Khan, retired upon the fort of Deenghur, situated in the Cholistan, about twenty koss distance from Bahawalpur, where he took up his quarters.

Considering his unaided efforts unequal to the forces of the Khan, he induced the Daoodputra Khans of Kheirpur, Kaempur, and Hasilpur, to combine with him in carrying on hostilities against Bahawal Khan. They accordingly bound themselves by a solemn oath and engagement to support each other. Having thus effected a union with them, he again went over personally to the chief of Bikaner to procure his quota of succour, which was readily furnished; and uniting this force with his own, he advanced on Majghur, where he halted.

Bahawal Khan at first tried to sow the seeds of dissension among the combined Khans; and with this view made overtures to Kareem Khan, one of the chief individuals of the league, but the latter turned a deaf ear to his persuasions; and he was, therefore, obliged to resort to hostile preparations.

While matters were thus far advanced, the public attention was drawn to an event of greater importance. Shah Zaman, who had given up his expedition to Hindustan on account of the internal commotions which broke out in his dominions, again marched out with a large army from Cabul, on his favourite expedition. By regular marches he arrived at Lahore, when all the Jaghirdars and local officers were summoned to wait on his majesty. The Mohammedans instantly obeyed the royal orders, and were introduced to an audience through the prime minister; but the Sikhs, entertaining great apprehensions for their safety, refused compliance, and to escape the royal anger, betook themselves to the wooded part of the country towards Chonian and Pakpatan. The king was highly displeased with their obstinacy, and issued a general proclamation for their indiscriminate massacre. Nezam-ud-Deen Khan, the chief of Kasur, from his intimate knowledge of the localities, was appointed the leader of a detachment of royal troops to their haunts, in order to annihilate them; but the Kasur chief gave wrong information from patriotic motives, and took care to avoid coming in contact with the intended victims. They therefore returned to Lahore, after a fruitless effort to accomplish his majesty's object.

About this period, the famous Runjeet Singh brought himself into notice by his bold irruptions. He had at this time a party of eight or nine hundred horse under his command, and carried on depredations around the royal camp with remarkable impunity. Such was the negligence and idleness of the king's army, that no one could arrest his movements—nay, such was the bad disposition prevailing among the king's own ministers, that instead of suppressing they rather encouraged the embarrassment.

Shir Mohammed Khan Durranee, the son of Shah Walee, Vizir of the late Ahmed Shah, stood high in Zaman's estimation. He was a clever man, and very popular among the Durranees. On one occasion, as he was speaking to his majesty on some important subject, Rahmutullah, the prime minister, was so moved by his jealous feelings, that he indiscreetly struck him in the face. Shir Mohammed, considering the opportunity unfavourable to return the insult as it deserved, took it patiently; but his feelings were so much offended, that he secretly encouraged Runjeet Singh, as well as other Sikh chiefs, to continue to harrass the royal camp with their incursions, assuring them at the same time, that the king was not disposed to continue long in the country.

Emboldened by such favourable intelligence, the Sikhs commenced infesting the camp in every quarter, and scarcely a day passed in which they did not carry away horses or other property. Supplies were also cut off in their way to the camp; and thus great embarrassment was caused among the royal troops.

In this emergency, Nezam-ud-Deen, the Kasur ruler, offered to the Vizir to punish the Sikhs, if he were provided with ten thousand horses. To try his fidelity, the king first ordered him to send some of his own men on a foraging party. He readily submitted to the royal order; and as the party was returning with forage from Kut-Lukhput, about five koss distant from Lahore, they were attacked by Runjeet Singh, at the head of four hundred Sawars. The Kasurees behaved bravely; and although almost all of them were wounded on the occasion, they did not allow the Sikhs to possess themselves of the forage. The skirmish continued till after sunset, when Runjeet Singh was compelled by the darkness to retreat.

The Shah was highly pleased with the conduct of Nezam-ud-Deen's men, and indicated his pleasure by conferring a Khelat on the Khan. His majesty was well disposed to have employed him on similar expeditions, had he not been obliged to return immediately to Cabul, on the breaking out of fresh commotions in that part of his territory, occasioned by the insurrection of Mohammed.

In the following year, Sadik, the Khan's second son, was favoured by the birth of a son, who was named Raheem-Yar, afterwards Bhawal Khan the Third, who now occupies the throne.

Mukdoom Hamed of Uch, who had been confined within his house, again began to stir up a rebellion. He was joined this time by Hajji Khan, of the Mehdanee tribe, and by Ikhtyar Khan, as well as other Daoodputra Khans in that quarter. Sadik Khan was selected in consequence by the Khan, to proceed at the head of a large force, to suppress this as well as the insurrection of the Marufanee chief.

On his arrival at Bahawalpur, he was joined by his younger brother, Feizullah Khan, who had lately been deputed to Multan to apply for aid to the governor of that province, as well as to entertain some mercenaries. Owing to the ancient friendship existing between the latter and the Khan, he was received and treated hospitably by Muzuffir Khan; and was on his departure furnished with a party of Multan troops, under the command of one of his own officers. He then returned with this detachment, as well as the levy which he himself had raised, in time to effect a junction with his elder brother.

The Khan, in order to gain time while making hostile preparations, had opened overtures of peace with Khoda Buksh, which occupied nearly two months, but without success.

Tired of long inactivity, the troops of Khoda Buksh now began to destroy the produce of the country, and commit other outrages on the Ryots of Bahawalpur, along the left bank of the river. This brought them in collision with Sadik's forces, and a severe contest followed; in which, by some misfortune, the gunpowder magazine of the young Khan took fire in the midst of the fight, and many of his men were killed by the explosion. Gholam Murtwa, one of the chief officers, was also among those who were destroyed by this accident. Some other officers were also slain and wounded by the fire of the enemy, which was sharply kept up during the whole time. Notwithstanding this misfortune, the Bahawalpur troops were not dispirited, but continued the fight most resolutely. The loss on the enemy's side was also great; and at last they gave way and took to flight. They were closely pursued by the victors, who obliged Khoda Buksh to beg for an amnesty through an agent, and to offer to wait on the young Khan in person, if he would give up the pursuit. His supplication was readily complied with, and the pursuing party was in consequence recalled.

A few days afterwards, Khoda Buksh, agreeably to his promise, made his appearance in Sadik's camp, to throw himself on the mercy of the Khan, who was so moved at the fate of his fallen enemy, that he not only pardoned him for his past conduct, but took him into favour for the future. Khoda Buksh continued in the Khan's court for some days, and was treated kindly; insomuch that one day, when on a shooting excursion, Bahawal Khan gave him a seat behind him on his own camel. He was, however, of a naturally rebellious disposition, and the conciliatory treatment which he received wrought no change in his mischievous desires. Pretending to go out for the purpose of shooting, he again made his escape to the Cholistan, and took refuge in the fortress of Majghur already in his possession.

Bahawal Khan now returned from Deirawer to Bahawalpur, and as usual was waited upon by the Daoodputra Khans, who came to pay their respects to him. A few days afterwards, he removed to Ahmedpur to look after his affairs in that quarter.

About this period, Shah Zaman moved to Candahar. A dispute, which was the foundation of the rapid decline of the Durranee monarchy, here broke out among his officers. Vafadar, the prime minister, was naturally a very selfish and avaricious man, and could not look upon the prosperity of his colleagues without feelings of jealousy. Sirdar Paenda Khan and Mohammed Azeem Khan Alukzaee, as well as some others, were the first objects of his envy. He showed his ill-will by recommending a reduction in their Jaghirs; but soon afterwards a better opportunity for indulging his spleen towards them offered itself.

A Fakeer, or pious devotee of the Sufee moralist sect,

named Gholam Mohammed, a native of Lahore, resided in Candahar, and was celebrated for his piety. His religious fame induced Fatteh Khan, the son of Paenda, and Mohammed Azeem, as well as two or three other Durranee chiefs, to enter themselves among his votaries (Moreeds). This circumstance spread the fame of the Fakeer far and wide, and excited numbers of people to include themselves among his followers. Even the king himself was impressed with the idea of his piety, and one night invited him to his presence and begged him to pronounce a benediction in his own behalf.

The approach of Gholam Mohammed, however, was not palatable to Vafadar, because he feared that he might speak to his majesty in a manner favourable to his rivals Paenda Khan, etc. He therefore set about getting rid of the Fakeer; and, with this view, he instigated the Mullahs or Mahomedan lawyers, to rise against him, on the pretence that he was a deist, and discountenanced the "Shara." The Mullahs accordingly brought the matter to the notice of the king; and, through the assistance of the Vizir, succeeded in obtaining an order for beheading their victim. So they excited a religious faction, to carry out the sentence. Mohammed Azeem Khan, to save the poor man from the fury of the fanatics, took him under his own protection.

The Mullahs complained of his conduct to Vafadar, who hereupon ordered Azeem either to deliver over the refugee to the Mullahs, or turn him out of Candahar, because his continuance there was considered a breach of the Shara or laws. The Fakeer was therefore escorted in safety by Azeem Khan's own Sawars to Shawl.

This circumstance, however, led him to form a conspiracy, in combination with Fatteh Khan, etc. against the life of the Vizir; but before it came to maturity, a servant of the latter, who was cognizant of the plot, secretly disclosed it to Vafadar. He immediately induced the informant to make a similar disclosure on the same night to his majesty, and to add, that it was also intended to murder the king himself.

In the impulse of the moment, the Shah ordered Paenda and other Ameers to appear at court *instantly*. The innocent Sirdar, although warned by his son, Fatteh Khan, nevertheless obeyed the royal command, in the consciousness of innocence. Azeem Khan and other Ameers also attended; and while they were in attendance, guards were placed over their houses. Fatteh Khan, who was in his house at the time, made his escape by climbing over the walls, while the Ameers were put in chains. In this state they continued till midnight, when they were all indiscriminately put to death.

Vafadar, however, did not consider his revenge fully gratified as long as Gholam Mohammed continued alive. He therefore immediately sent out a party of horsemen to trace and murder the poor Fakeer, who was found in Seiwee-Dader, and immediately beheaded, together with one of his disciples. Their heads were conveyed to Candahar to satisfy the sanguinary revenge of the Vizir.

From this period we may trace the decline of the Durranee empire. Almost all the Durranee chiefs were from that moment disaffected to the king, who was not at all ignorant of the disposition of his nobles. To divert their attention, therefore, he removed to Cabul, and leaving Shir Mohammed in charge of that province, continued his progress to Peshawur, apparently with the intention of renewing his expedition against Hindustan.

But the continuance of Fatteh Khan at large was a subject of constant consideration and anxiety to the Shah and his Vizir. Repeated orders were issued to the district officers for his apprehension; but nothing was heard of him until he appeared before Candahar with Prince Mohammed, and a party of five hundred horsemen. He made a night attack on the encampment of Kulee Khan Daroga, who was encamped within fifteen koss of that city, with a force amounting to twenty thousand horse and foot. The darkness of the night caused much confusion among them; and, leaving the whole encampment to be plundered by the invaders, they retired to Candahar.

The booty in horses and other property which thus fell into the hands of the Shahzada improved his circumstances so much, that he soon advanced to lay siege to Candahar, which was reduced in a few days. He then busied himself in equipping an army on a better and more extensive scale. Shah Zaman at this time was at Peshawur.

After the necessary preparations were accomplished, Mohammed moved out towards Cabul, while Shah Zaman on hearing of the fall of Candahar, also retired to that place. Without staying at Cabul, he continued his progress towards Candahar, sending in advance two Dustas or detachments of his army, under the command of two officers of rank. At the commencement of the next year, a letter was received from the advanced guard, announcing the desertion to the enemy of one of the commanding officers, and applying for reinforcements. The king therefore expedited his own march in that direction, but afterwards suddenly fell back on Cabul. The retreat caused much confusion in his camp, and induced his own troops, as well as those of the enemy, to plunder every thing in their way, and even to deprive the camp-followers also of all their *rights* and provisions.

Shah Zaman on his appearing before Cabul was refused admittance into the town by the governor, and was, in consequence, obliged to fly to Jelalabad with Vafadar, accompanied by only five of his own dependents.

Mohammed now made his entry into Cabul without resistance, and was immediately declared king; upon which he occupied the vacant throne. A party was sent out in pursuit of the fugitive Zaman to Jelalabad, where he was seized and deprived of both his eyes, while his Vizir was put to many excruciating tortures, and afterwards slain. The unfortunate king was then removed to Cabul, where a coin was struck in the name of Mohammed, and Fatteh Khan was invested with the office of prime minister.

A friendship had existed for some time past between the Khan and Paenda Khan; the new Vizir, therefore, to mark his sense of his father's friendship, not only obtained a Rakum of confirmation from the new king, in the name of Bahawal Khan, but also distinguished him still further, by conferring on him the title of "Muklis-ud-dola," with a valuable Khelat.

Khoda Buksh Khan, on his retreat to Majghur put forth all his strength to organise a rebellion on a more extensive scale than before. Mobarik Khan, as already stated, had been labouring under the displeasure of his father, Bahawal Khan; and to gain him over was considered of great importance to his purpose. He was not disappointed; for their mutual interests induced them to enter into a combination. The Mukdoom Sahib of Uch, as well as Hajji Khan, another disaffected noble, was likewise not backward in the common cause, while the Rajah of Bikaner, his old friend, did not scruple to afford him his usual quota of assistance. With their united troops, Khoda Buksh intended to surprise Bahawalpur.

Bahawal Khan, however, being aware of his combination, in order to frustrate his object, equipped a large force, under the command of Mohammed Sadik, at Deirawer, and immediately despatched it to protect the capital.

Meanwhile Khoda Buksh, accompanied by the Bikaner auxiliary force, as well as the other combined troops, marched by way of Paukul and Majghur to Kaempur, which was situated within thirty-three koss to the east of Bahawalpur. Here he encamped; and to make his party as strong as possible, he induced the Daoodputra Khans of the neighbourhood to support his cause. Bahawal Khan also, on hearing of the increasing strength of the rebels, despatched another detachment under some chosen officers, to join his son.

While preparations were thus being made on both sides, Mobarik remained under restraint in the fort of Deirawer. To effect his escape, Khoda Buksh secretly sent out a party of fifty Sawars, under the superintendence of his own Kidmutghar (waiter), and a Daoodputra chief, named Dilawer, while he himself moved to Deenghur to await his arrival. On their approach, the Sawars were concealed at a distance behind heaps of sand, while the leaders, under the pretence of selling firewood, continued to make their way, in broad day-light, into the gate of the fort, with a camel laden with the article of their pretended trade. They then contrived, by means of a menial, to inform Mobarik of their arrival.

Mobarik, who was an ambitious character, and only waited for such an opportunity, immediately escaped from the fort unobserved, and mounting a camel, set off for Deenghur, where he safely joined the camp, in company with Dilawer. His arrival infused fresh life into Khoda Buksh and his followers, and they gave expression to their joy by beating drums, etc. The young Khan was instantly declared the ruler of the country, and placed on the Musnud, upon which, every one present in the camp tendered him homage, by undergoing the usual ceremony of making Mujra, or obeisance. After the ceremony of proclaiming Mobarik was over, they moved out to Majghur, and from thence back to Kaempur. A council was held with the chief Daoodputras, as to what was the next thing to be done, when they all unanimously agreed that their arrangements were not complete until they were joined by the Mukdoom Sahib, and Hajji Khan of the Gurhee Ikhtyar Khan. To gain the assistance of the latter, Khoda Buksh openly communicated with him in person from the fortress of Deenghur. Hajji Khan, to give a better colour to his design, waited on the Khan, and advised him to compromise matters, and offered his own mediation for the purpose. The Khan was not indisposed to such a proposition, and permitted him to quell the insurrection if possible. The Hajji accordingly proceeded to Deenghur to open the pretended negotiations with Khoda Buksh, who was by this time joined by the Mukdoom of Uch. Here they held a council concerning the confirmation of Mobarik to the exclusion of his father; and on his return, the Hajji imposed on the credulity of the Khan, by stating that he had persuaded Khoda Buksh to relinquish the rebellion. After this, he returned to his own home, where he was joined by the Mukdoom at the head of his party, and they directed their united exertions to exciting the ill-will of the Ryots against their sovereign.

The Khan, however, was not long ignorant of their mischievous designs. To oppose their further progress, he sent a detachment of his troops under the command of Taj Mohammed, Sultan Mohammed, and Mohammed, three trustworthy officers; while the command of the force to be conducted against his rebellious son was conferred on Sadik, his favourite son, who had for his adviser Beharjee, the chief officer. Mobarik, on hearing of his brother's movements, departed from Deenghur, and proceeded with all his partizans towards Bahawalpur, and he encamped within a koss to the south of that city.

While these movements were going on, the party that was sent against Hamed, etc. came into collision with the rebels so suddenly that they could not avoid fighting before they were prepared for it. Taj Khan, one of the chief officers, having been shot dead by a musket ball, the troops gave way and fled. Although the loss in killed and wounded, as well as in the loss of horses, was great on the part of the Khan, yet the victory was not easily gained by the insurgents. Hajji Khan, the leader, was severely wounded, and many others on his side were also slain. He was immediately removed to his fortress; while the Mukdoom, with his surviving followers, joined Mobarik.

Flushed with victory, the insurgents became still bolder than before; and a party of Bikaner troops was next sent out to lay waste the country along the bank of the river. They carried on their depredations with impunity to within seven koss of Bahawalpur, as far as the temple of Saed Mohkam; but, as they were returning with the booty which they had acquired by plundering the poor Ryots, they came upon a party of Sadik's troops which were lying in wait in a Nullah. The enemy met with a very warm reception; the contest became general, and much blood was shed on both sides, until the darkness of the night put an end to the conflict.

In the morning of the 19th of Ramzan, 1214, A. H., (A.D. 1799), the two armies were again drawn up in battle array, and hostilities were renewed with great violence on both sides, the enemy being joined by the rest of the troops. The action was maintained for some time, and a great number were killed on either side. Among the latter, were Kamal on the part of Mobarik, and Keisur on that of the other party, the two principal officers. At length fortune decided the day in favour of Sadik, and his rebellious brother was eventually put to flight.

In order to elude pursuit, Mobarik, together with his

protector, Khoda Buksh, and some other Daoodputra Khans, made the best of their way to Bikaner, where they were hospitably and kindly received; while Hamed returned to his own residence in Uch.

The Mukdoom Sahib, failing in his hostile movements, now endeavoured to indulge his revenge by stratagem. He engaged two persons, named Gule Beg and Jeiwan, to assassinate the Khan, and secretly sent them to the fort of Deirawer where he was residing. On their arrival, they took up their residence outside the walls of the town in a Tukya, or house of a Fakeer, and watched for a favourable opportunity of effecting their purpose. On one occasion, as the Khan was returning from a pleasure excursion in the evening, they joined the train of his Sawaree; Gule Beg among the Sawars, and the other among the falconers. The former, however, was seized with fear, and did not therefore attempt any thing; but the latter, being still firm in his murderous design, went close up to the palanquin of the Khan as far as the gateway, where his strange appearance attracted the notice of the porter, who prevented him from entering the fort. This check defeated his diabolical object. Furious with anger and despair, he attacked and wounded the porter with a sabre; but before he had time to repeat the blow, he was killed by a Poorbia Sipahi who was close by. His last words were:—" A hundred thanks that I have fallen a martyr to a noble cause; but it is very mortifying that my accomplice was not punctual in his assistance." With these words he breathed his last. The sword which was found about him, was recognised to have borne the peculiar impression with which other arms belonging to the Mukdoom were marked. This circumstance raised strong suspicions in the Khan's mind; and hence his hatred and displeasure towards that individual were still further excited.

It appears that Nasir Khan, the son of Alum Khan Korkeich, who on the death of his father had returned to Bahawal Khan's court, and had been retaken into favour, had again retired from some private cause. His brother Kheir Mohammed now waited on the Khan, and through his intercession Nasir was recalled and reinstated in his appointment. A few days afterwards the two brothers were despatched to demolish the fortress of Tatta, belonging to Mukdoom Sahib. They succeeded in performing this service to the great satisfaction of the Khan, and returned to the court on the 2nd of Zekad, 1204 A. H. (A.D. 1789).

On the demolition of the fortress, Hamed did not consider it safe to continue at Uch; and accordingly he removed with his family and followers to Jalalpur Khakyan. Thence he deputed Salamut Rae to Muzuffir Khan, with a request that he would show favour to his deplorable state. The governor was moved with pity at his fallen state, and consequently marched out to Shujahabad to see what he could do in his behalf. On his arrival there, he sent out Mohammed Surfaraz Khan to meet the Mukdoom, and to give him every consolation, but to temporise with him with regard to the aid he asked. He was, however, soon tired of the evasive course pursued by the governor, and in disgust moved to his village named Sanker, whence he returned after a few days to Jalalpur.

About this time Sheikh Kumr-ud-Deen, who was employed for some time as an agent in the Durranee Court, on the part of Meean Abdunnabee, joined the Mukdoom, and soon succeeded in gaining an ascendancy in his councils. He advised him to proceed to Dereh Deenpanah; and, in order to make Abdussamed, the manager of that district, further interested in his master's behalf, he induced the latter to supply him with four thousand gold mohurs, to enable him to raise troops for his service. His avarice, however, conquered his integrity; and, instead of expending the money as promised, he employed it for his own private use. The Mukdoom being thus entirely disappointed in his object in this quarter, moved to Dereh Ghazi Khan; but being unsuccessful there also, he went on to Methan-Kot. On crossing over the river, he was detained a few days in the village of Milsean, on account of the sudden death of his son, Fazul Ali, whose loss he lamented most bitterly. After this he proceeded to Kaderpur, and to the Gurhee of Ikhtyar Khan.

Here he was advised by his old friend, Hajji Khan, to make peace with the Khan. The proposition was readily embraced, and Hajji accordingly mediated a negotiation between the two parties; and after this patched-up reconciliation Hamed returned to Uch.

Such hurried negotiations, however, did not last long; for hardly had three months elapsed since his return, when the Mukdoom was again seized with so dreadful a fit, that he would sometimes pursue his own men with a drawn sword. Thus excited, he again betook himself to his wild schemes, and leaving Uch in charge of his two servants, Ali Morad and Behareedas, he moved to

Ramkolee, his own village, with his Harem, and Abbas Ali, his son. From this place he again began to infest the vicinity of Ahmedpur; but his depredations were soon checked by a party of troops sent by the Khan to protect that town.

This failure led him to depute his confidential servant, Muzuffir Ali, with orders amounting to a considerable sum, together with a valuable Persian sword, to the court of Jodhpoor, in order to try, through the interposition of Abdunnabee, whether he could not induce the chief of that country to favour his cause; and, in case of failure, to go on to Bikaner, with similar views. The agent, however, was not successful in his mission in either of these courts.

Meanwhile, the persons who were left in charge of Uch, disloyally betrayed that place into the hands of Bahawal Khan, and entered his service.

These repeated reverses of fortune further excited the fury of the already despairing Hamed. He now employed himself most industriously in creating disturbances in the Khan's territory, the suppression of which became imperatively necessary on the Khan. With this view, a detachment of troops was sent out against him, under the command of Hamed Khan Marufanee, with two other officers of the Daoodputra tribe. They at once proceeded to lay siege to Ramkolee, where Hamed had shut himself up on their approach, and a bloody contest, in which many lives were lost on both sides, was the consequence. At last, finding his position rather difficult to be maintained, he contrived to escape on the morning of the 15th Ramzan, 1215 A. H. (A. D. 1800), taking with him at the same time his son, the rest of his family, and all his moveables by water to Kaderpur, where he took up his quarters.

In the same year, Abdunnabee growing disaffected with the cold treatment of his host, the chief of Jodhpur, once more brought his grievances under the notice of the Durranee monarch, through the medium of Letafet Ali, a Khoja or eunuch. This man was originally a slave of the Meean, but having obtained his liberty, he had proceeded from Leiya on a pilgrimage to Mecca, and on his return, had succeeded in getting service with Mohammed Shah. The Khoja, moved with emotions of gratitude to his late master, exerted his best efforts to induce his majesty to have pity on his miserable fate, and he at last succeeded in getting the district of Rojhan, one of the dependencies of Dereh Ghazi Khan, to be conferred in Jaghir on Abdunnabee. Accordingly, the Meean, on the receipt of the Sanud, despatched his son, Fazul Ali, with his mother, to take charge of the Jaghir.

He was, however, soon after visited with a serious misfortune. His house accidentally taking fire, the whole of his valuable jewels and property were reduced to ashes, and only one ornament of pearl escaped destruction. This gem he pledged to a banker for 40,000 rupees, to enable him to depart from Jodhpur. On his way, he passed the fort of Deirawer, where he was received and treated with proper honours by the Khan.

About the same time, Mobarik, leaving the court of Bikaner, proceeded to Jeyselmeer. Although he was received with consideration, he did not remain, but proceeded to the house of his father-in-law, Fazul Khan

Peerhanee, who, regardless of the close tie which bound them, sent him away to the Khan, who put him in confinement.

In this year, deputations were exchanged between the Khan and the chief of Bikaner, with a view to restore peace. The return deputation which the Rajah sent, consisted of Doulut Rae, Sawaee Shah, Khoda Buksh Marufanee, and Taleb Khan. After accomplishing the object of their mission, they took leave in order to return, when Doulut Rae, who was formerly in the service of the Khan, chose to remain behind. This gave occasion to the abrupt breaking up of the negotiations so recently set on foot; and the irritated Rajah, excited by Khoda Buksh, immediately ordered his troops under the command of Sawaee Shah and Taleb Khan to be assembled at Deenghur, situated in the Cholistan, with a view of renewing hostilities. The Khan also despatched a party of 3,000 horse and foot, commanded by Azmet Khan, to encamp on the frontier, near the fort of Peerhanee, to watch the movements of the enemy. The latter, however, one day succeeded in driving away the cattle belonging to the Bahawalpur territory; but they were pursued in time, and the cattle recovered.

While these petty quarrels were going on in this quarter, Khoda Buksh Khan had penetrated into the interior, taking the fortress of Pholehra, etc. His progress was, however, arrested beyond Kheirpur by the arrival of Sadik with many chief officers and a considerable force. The latter was instructed by his father not to proceed further than Lalsohara; but Nasir Khan Korkeich, not minding the instructions, although prevented by the young Khan, went on further. The two forces thus came into collision, and hostilities commenced; but they terminated in mutual peace. On the 14th of Safer, 1216 A. H. (A. D. 1801), the Bahawalpur troops returned to the capital.

A mint was established in this year at Bahawalpur, and silver and gold coins were struck in the name of Mohammed Shah.

In the same year, Behram Ali, with his two nephews, Mohammed Yar and Ahmed Yar, who were also not well-disposed towards the Khan, was seized and thrown into prison in the fort of Mobarikpur.

About this time, the Mukdoom interested in his behalf Meer Sohrab Khan of Talpur, and induced him to intercede with Bahawal Khan in his cause. With this view, the latter deputed Abdurrahman his agent to the Khan's court, whence he was dismissed with favourable answers.

The ascendancy of Fatteh Khan in the councils of Mohammed Shah occasioned the promotion of Afghans in his majesty's court. Meer Alum Khan Noorzaee having been nominated the governor of Dereh Ghazi Khan, at this time arrived in the Dereh, and assumed the charge of his government. Abdussamed, also another Afghan of the Badozaee tribe, the Jaghirdar of Dereh Deenpanah, was appointed governor of Multan, to succeed Muzuffir Khan. He was furnished with royal orders addressed to the Khans, directing them respectively to assist him in taking possession of his government, as well as the governors of Derehjats. He forwarded them to the addresses on his approach; while he himself, on his arrival at his Jaghir, set about making warlike preparations. Thence he addressed a letter to the Khan, offering to deliver the fort of Khanghur in perpetuity to him, if he would assist him in occupying Multan. At the same time, a deputation arrived on the part of Muzuffir Khan, to sue for aid against his enemy. The Khan assured him of every succour in his power; and moreover sent an embassy in return, under Gosaeen Behar Rae, in acknowledgment of his good offices.

The Khan was as good as his word; for he soon after equipped a force of 5,000 horse and foot, and when everything was ready despatched it across the river, under the command of Jewan Ram Munshee, with other Daoodputra officers; viz., Deen Mohammed Khan, Jamaree, and Abdullah Khan Tapanee, etc. etc. But, without waiting for their arrival, Muzuffir Khan had already despatched the greater portion of his troops under the command of Gholam Murtwa Suddoozye and Khan Mohammed, the father-in-law of Zulfikar Khan, to lay siege to Deenpur, where Abdussamed had shut himself up.

In this emergency, Abdussamed had applied for aid to Meer Alum, the governor of Dereh Ghazi Khan, who at first tried to adjust the matter, by amicably deputing Kareem Khan, his servant, to the Nawab; but failing in this point, on account of the harsh proceedings of his agent, he despatched 1,000 well-disciplined Sawars to aid his friend. Encouraged by the junction of this force, Abdussamed made a bold sally and attacked the besiegers. A severe struggle ensued, and at last the latter were repulsed with a loss of 220 men.

Notwithstanding the repulse of the besiegers, the victory was not decisive. In order to prepare himself better for further operations, Abdussamed removed his family to Deenpanah; and, in the meantime, the Multan force having been joined by the Daoodputra troops, he returned to the siege. In a short time the combined forces levelled the fort to the ground, and Abdussamed was obliged to seek safety in flight.

Since the expulsion of Mobarik Hajji Khan, the chief of the Gurhee had remained quiet; but the present state of affairs now gave him another opportunity of shewing his malice towards his feudal lord. Meer Alum was considered the best instrument to serve his end; and with this view he courted his friendship through his own Vakeel, as well as his confidential servant, Kareem Khan.

The friendly alliance established between these two individuals naturally excited the jealousy and fear of Bahawal Khan; and to punish Alum Khan was therefore considered of the first importance. An army, consisting of 7,000 men, was immediately despatched across the river, under the command of Abdullah Khan and Dewan Salamut Rae. On entering the province of Dereh Ghazi Khan, they first directed their arms against the fort of Candahar, which had been lately built by Alum, near Mohammedpur; but, on their approach, they were met by Munsoor, the officer of Alum Khan. He was, however, unable to withstand the bravery of the troops, and was compelled to make a hurried retreat.

On 18th Rajab, 1217 A. H. (A.D. 1802), letters were received by the Khan from the governors of Multan and

Kheichee, recommending a combination of their arms against the common foe, Alum. The Khan readily agreed to the proposal, and despatched his son Nasir with an additional force to effect a junction with the army already in the field. The Multan and Kheichee armies, the one under the command of Zulfikar Khan and the other under that of Mohammed Khan, also assembled in the village of Ajub Walah. The three armies having effected a union, crossed the Indus from this place on boats, and advanced on the Dereh. Alum Khan also marched out at the head of his troops to meet them in the field; but feeling his inability to oppose the united forces, he retired without hazarding a battle to Jampur, and thence by way of Haread to Candahar. After this, the campaign broke up, and the three armies returned to their respective quarters.

Having accomplished the expulsion of Alum, the Khan now directed his attention towards his old but now weakened enemy, Hajji Khan. A considerable force was accordingly sent across the river to attack the strongholds of Hajji, who was defeated and put to flight in a skirmish. The invaders then proceeded to lay siege to Sahenwala, one of his strongest haunts. During the siege, Salamut Rae, the chief officer of the Khan, was struck dead by a ball from the fort; but the garrison could not hold out long, and eventually surrendered the place at discretion. The fort of Noushehra, which was occupied by Islam Khan Daoodputra, was also reduced without much difficulty. After these captures, the victorious troops recrossed the Indus at Methan-Kot, on their return to Bahawalpur; but their progress was interrupted by the sudden appearance of Hajji Khan, with the intention of stopping them. This circumstance having been brought to the notice of the Khan, a party of 2,000 horse was immediately sent off, under the command of Fatteh Mohammed Ghoree, to attack the rear of the enemy. The Hajji, however, finding his position between the two forces untenable, soon gave way and returned to Khanpür, whither he was followed and attacked by the Bahawalpur troops. He was obliged to quit that place also; and, as the only course left, he proceeded direct to Bahawalpur, and threw himself on the mercy of the Khan, by whom he was most generously pardoned, and restored to his Jaghir.

The expulsion of Alum gave a reason for the nomination of another Afghan as his successor; and, accordingly, in 1218 A. H. (A. D. 1803), Ata Mohammed Khan, son of Ahmed Khan Noorzaee, having obtained the governorship of Dereh Ghazi, arrived in that place, but owing to the dethronement of Mohammed Shah, his career was not of long duration.

Soon after his accession at Candahar, Shuja-ul-Mulk set out on an expedition against Sindh, and on his way was joined by Abdunnabee. On hearing of his advance, Meer Gholam Ali, the ruler of the country, also busied himself in collecting his scattered troops; but before coming to a battle, he tried to pacify the monarch by loyal overtures. With that intention, Meer Ismael, the son of Ibrahim Shah, a Persian, was selected for the mission; his old Vakeel having destroyed himself in consequence of a removal from his post. It appears that his embassy had the desired effect; because soon afterwards a deputation consisting of Akrum Khan Allizaee, an officer of high rank, and Meer Mohammed, the ruler of Khelat, returned with him to Gholam Ali, and matters were compromised, by the latter having agreed to pay a Nuzrana of fourteen lakhs of rupees to his majesty.

Immediately after the accomplishment of the above peace, the king bent his course to Rajonpur, where he was waited upon by Hajji Khan, and the Mukdoom of Uch, besides Fazul Ali and Islam Khan, who were also Daoodputras. Doulut Rae, at the same time, attended the Durbar as agent on the part of the Khan, and was soon afterwards followed by a deputation, consisting of Kader Buksh, his son, in conjunction with Hafiz Azeem Khan, and Mehrab-Korkeich, as well as Mohammed Beg and Subah Rae Munshee. After performing the usual ceremonies, the embassy returned to Bahawalpur.

On the former restoration of Hajji Khan's Jaghir, a part of it had been withheld by the Khan. The presence of the king was considered a favourable opportunity to recover this also; and at his request, Ahmed Khan Noorzaee was appointed by his majesty to see him put in possession of the estate which he claimed. The fortress of Dhaka, etc. situated on the right bank of the river, was also taken from the Khan's people, and made over to the charge of the Hajji.

The conduct of Hajji Khan again irritated the feelings of Bahawal Khan against him; and he accordingly took the earliest opportunity of gratifying his revenge. A large force was again sent out, commanded by Nasir and Kheir Mohammed Korkeich, together with two other officers of the Dheir tribe, to lay siege to his

Gurhee; and the operations were prolonged for nearly three months, when Hajji Khan, feeling his inability to defend the place any longer, again threw himself on the mercy of the Khan, and was pardoned.

Surat Sing, the chief of Bikaner, had long been anxious to get possession of the fort of Khanghur, which was situated in the Cholistan, and belonged to the Khan. Perceiving that an open attempt might not prove successful, he hit upon a stratagem to effect his purpose. A party of his troops, commanded by Rawet Ketsea, a Jaghirdar of Jeyselmeer, were despatched in the disguise of grain and cotton-dealers. They concealed their arms in the bales of their pretended goods, and in this manner effected an entrance into the fort. By some contrivance they also succeeded in distributing opium to some of the garrison, which entirely stupified them. When thus rendered powerless, they were of course easily subdued, so that some were killed on the spot, and others obliged to fly. Being wrongly informed that some treasure was buried under the walls of the fort, the victors next proceeded to level them to the ground; but they were totally disappointed, as nothing was found.

On being apprised of the reduction of the fort, the Khan lost no time in despatching a detachment of his troops, under the command of Abdullah Khan and Fatteh Mohammed Ghoree, on whose approach the place was evacuated, and subsequently reoccupied by the Khan's people.

From Dereh Ghazi Khan, Shah Shuja proceeded to Peshawur, and thence sent out an expedition against Kashmeer, under the management of the Vizir-ud-Doula (Ata Mohammed). The country was traversed and taken possession of without much difficulty, and soon afterwards the Vizir returned to court with an immense treasure which he acquired in the expedition.

In the following year, another expedition was despatched against Multan, under the command of the son of Ata Mohammed. On his arrival, he laid siege to the place; but Muzuffir Khan, feeling his own inability singly to oppose the royal troops, applied for aid to the Khan; and matters were compromised without further hostilities, through the interposition of Azeem Khan and some other officers of the Khan, who were despatched for the purpose.

The indulgence with which the Khan had twice treated Hajji Khan had no effect on his turbulent mind; and another event which excited his long-cherished enmity, occurred about this period.

Fazul Ali Khan Daoodputra, of the Holanee tribe, had lately engaged to marry his daughter to the Khan; but no sooner was the betrothment contracted, than, owing to his faithlessness, it was broken off. Considering his continuance in the vicinity of Bahawalpur rather unsafe from this cause, he divided his estate among his sons, while he himself proceeded towards Abhar. On the site of the original Abhar, which had for years remained in ruins, he laid the foundation of the present fortification, which, when finished, he converted into his residence. At the same time a friendly alliance was established between him and Hajji Khan. Fazul Ali, however, did not long remain in the peaceful enjoyment of his new acquisition. A pretender soon arose against him in the person of Islam Khan Gehranee, who succeeded in capturing Methan-Kot from the hands of his people without much resistance. Mohammed Khan, the son of Fazul Ali, who was located in Bhagseer, on hearing of this reverse, immediately set out with all his available Sawars, to oppose the invaders; but, as rash proceedings are very seldom successful, no sooner had he come into collision with his opponent, than he was repulsed, and obliged to seek security behind the walls of Benkula. Islam, encouraged by victory, lost no time in taking advantage of it, but proceeded to lay siege to the fort, and after a few days succeeded in capturing it.

In this emergency, Fazul Ali applied for aid to the Khan; and the latter, in compliance with his request, kindly sent out to assist him a party of his troops, under the command of Nasir Khan Korkeich, on whose approach, Islam Khan, feeling his incapacity to resist, voluntarily relinquished his newly-acquired possessions, which were restored to Fazul Ali; and the party returned to Bahawalpur without meeting with any opposition.

But as favours conferred on those who are naturally of a wicked disposition are seldom productive of a good effect, so, notwithstanding the marked and benevolent consideration of the Khan towards Fazul Ali, he entered into a league against his benefactor; and the confederated chiefs Hajji Khan, the Mukdoom Sahib, and Vadeereh Mohammed Khan, of Mohammedpur, assembled at his residence to consult as to the best mode of proceeding. The great avarice of Fazul Ali now got the better of his favourite scheme,—the valuable property in the possession of the Mukdoom was too tempting to be resisted,—and he determined to deprive him of it by force; but before his plan was matured, it came to the ears of the Mukdoom, who, to his great disappointment, instantly retired to his own territory.

The retirement of the Mukdoom, however, did not interfere with the original design of Fazul Ali; and he and Hajji Khan bound themselves by solemn engagements, conjointly to carry it out. Their attention was first drawn to the fortress of Sirdarghur, a distant and isolated position, situated in the Cholistan; and on the 14th Mohurrum, 1221 A. H. (A. D. 1806), they proceeded with their forces against the place. After some few days, the fort was surrendered by the governor, who was unable to defend it.

On being apprised of the fall of this fortress, the Khan lost no time in despatching a force consisting of fifteen thousand horse and foot, under the command of Nasir Khan and Fatteh Khan Ghoree, to lay waste the invader's own territory. Siege was immediately laid to the Gurhee of Hajji Khan. The place was well defended, and a party of the garrison soon attempted to expel them; but they were obliged to retire with some loss in killed and wounded, including two officers of note. The defence was nevertheless vigorously maintained; and although one of their officers of rank named Kheir Mohammed Korkeich, was struck dead by a musket ball, on the part of the besiegers, during the operations, the siege was prolonged till the last day of the Mohurrum, on which day the besieged again put themselves in battle array outside the walls of the fortress. A very bloody contest ensued; and at length they were again obliged to retire within the fort. As the siege was prolonged much more than was expected,—owing, perhaps, to the want of soldiers regularly trained to besieging,—the Khan sent out a reinforcement, commanded by Ghanee Mohammed and Rajaram, with instructions to throw up a bulwark close to the Gurhee, which might enable them to open a fire upon it with better effect, and at the same time secure them from the fire of the enemy, to which they had been incessantly exposed. A fortification was accordingly constructed in a short time near the Gurhee. The besiegers were also encouraged by Bahawal Khan with various marks of honour; and their operations were henceforward carried on with greater resolution and better success than before. Many of the buildings inside of the Gurhee were destroyed by cannonade, and the besieged were in consequence much disheartened, while Yusuf Khan, the brother of Fazul Ali, despairing of further defence, abandoned his post, and retired to Sultanpur, his own village. His example was followed by his other brother, Sultan Khan, as well as by many of the garrison. Fazul Ali who, together with his colleague Hajji, had joined them during the operations, had no other alternative left but to appear personally in the presence of Fatteh Mohammed Khan, the commander of the Khan's force, and sue for peace. His request was readily granted, on condition of the surrender of the Gurhee and payment of two lakhs of rupees in cash, besides the annual payment, in perpetuity, of half the product of his remaining possessions.

On the 9th of Ramzan in the same year, the Gurhee

was delivered over to the besiegers, as was stipulated when Hajji Khan was taken prisoner; but he died the next day in confinement.

At the same time, Fazul Ali, to complete his reconciliation with the irritated Khan, also gave him his daughter in marriage, as was originally arranged.

Before we proceed further with the history of Bahawal Khan, it is necessary to give an account of the Jodhpur chiefs,—to take a retrospective view of the history of Bujji Sing and his successors, the chiefs of Jodhpur,—which throws important light on the part which Bahawal Khan subsequently took in the affairs of that country.

Bujji Sing had a slave girl, named Golab, of uncommon beauty. With this woman he fell in love, and had by her a son, whom, at the request of his mistress, he declared heir apparent. The measure was disapproved of by his officers; but the untimely death of this favourite son decided the point without any dispute. Golab, an ambitious woman, who was quite sensible of the position and consequence she had acquired in the court on account of her late son, immediately supplied his place by adopting Shir Sing, another son of Bujji Sing by one of his favourite wives, and declared him the successor of her deceased child, while, by degrees, she obtained possession of the public treasure and the fort of Jodhpur. These events raised her fortune to the highest pitch, and she was now generally looked upon as the first person of influence in the court. She appears to have had a good taste for architecture; for the tank which is known by the name of Golab Sada was dug by her; and she also planted a garden, with a handsome building, beside a stupendous Hindoo temple, which is situated close to the town.

Her rising power had naturally given much offence to the Omras; but they waited for an opportunity to give vent to their disaffection. At last one of them, Sawae Sing, the Jaghirdar of Pokren, had the temerity to murder her in cold blood. To escape from the revenge of her provoked paramour, Bheim Sing, his grandson was at once declared ruler of the country, to the exclusion of his grandfather.

This revolution gave rise to a prolonged civil war between Bujji Sing and his grandson, till at length the latter was removed, with the whole of his treasures and valuables, to Pokren, and the ex-chief was restored, on condition, that on his death he was to be succeeded by Bheim Sing.

Meanwhile Shir Sing, the heir apparent, died, leaving a son named Maun Sing. His death was shortly followed by that of Bujji Sing himself; and this event, as originally stipulated, occasioned the restoration of Bheim Sing to the throne of Jodhpur. His succession was, however, disputed by Maun Sing, and they had several battles among themselves; but the death of Bheim Sing decided the point in favour of Maun Sing, who was soon after recalled by the Omras to Jodhpur, and raised to the vacant Musnud.

In Sawae Sing, the protector of Bheim Sing, Maun Sing had, however, a formidable foe. He exerted himself strenuously to sow the seeds of disaffection in the breasts of the army and Ryots towards him. But, in the meantime, an event occurred which tended, in a great measure, to favour his rebellion.

On the death of Bheim Sing, his wife, the niece of Jagat Sing the ruler of Jypur, who was pregnant, had returned home to her uncle; and, in the course of time, gave birth to a son, afterwards named Dhonkel Sing.

In him Sawae Sing found a good pretender for Jodhpur, and at the same time raised the ambition of his uncle Jagat Sing, by telling him, that as Dhonkel Sing was a minor, and could not therefore assume the charge of the government until he had attained his majority, he was the proper person to be appointed regent during his minority. Jagat Sing was too ambitious to resist such inviting temptations; and he accordingly assembled a large army, consisting of his own men and of auxiliaries. He then invaded the Jodhpur territories, and laid siege to the capital, accompanied by his allies Surat Sing of Bikaner, and Sawae Sing.

At this time Maun Sing deputed his minister, Indoraj, to Bahawalpur, to solicit the assistance of Bahawal Khan in the prosecution of the war. The minister was received and treated with civility, but was soon dismissed, apparently without the solicited aid.

The distress attendant on a lengthened siege, suggested to Maun Sing the necessity of causing dissension among his enemies. Ameer Khan, the Tonk chief, with about 40,000 horse and foot, was in the pay of Jagat Sing, and his predatory bands overran and destroyed all the country round. Through the interposition of Madhojee Sindhia, Indoraj induced the Pathan to separate himself from the besiegers, and enter the service of Maun Sing. He was now employed in laying waste the lands in the Jypur territory; and in this way he compelled Jagat Sing to raise the siege and to return to his capital. While, to get rid of Surat Sing, his ally, Indoraj, tempted some of his servants by the promise of Jaghirs to give him poison in his meals. The symptoms of poison soon after began to exhibit themselves, and the Rajah became insensible. In this state he was hurried on to Bikaner, where his pulse ceased to beat. Taking him for dead, his son, Ruttun Sing, was raised by his officers to the Musnud; and after this ceremony, the body of his father was removed to the outside of the town for the purpose of being burned, as customary, when, to the great surprise of those assembled, his pulse began to revive, and in a short time he was restored to life and to his throne.

Notwithstanding the return of the threatening army, Sawae Sing still continued in arms, and occupied Nagor and other places in that quarter, while the fort of Taladee was taken possession of by the Bikaner Chief.

Indoraj, the minister of Maun Sing, again waited on Bahawal Khan, and entreated him to assist his master in rescuing the above forts. In compliance with his request, the Khan sent off a large force, commanded by Gul Mohammed Korkeich and Abdurraheem, to Jodhpur.

After visiting Maun Sing, the Daoodputra force marched against Taladee, which was captured without much opposition, and restored to the Rajah. They also occupied three other fortresses belonging to Bikaner; namely, Phakra, Meerghur, and Maratha, situated in the Cholistan. This success struck great consternation into the mind of Sawae Sing; and, to avoid coming into contact with the Daoodputras, he shut himself up in the fort of Bikaner. After this, the Bahawalpur troops returned to their own country.

Ameer Khan, who had some long-standing pecuniary claims against the Jodhpur state, urged a speedy adjustment; and the government not being able to satisfy his demands, Indoraj, the minister, was put into confinement, and was soon after slain in an affray which ensued, owing to the insolent conduct of his troops. Maun Sing was so much affected and alarmed at this unwarrantable proceeding of the Pathan, that he immediately became a recluse, and resigned the "Raj" in favour of his son, Chatur Sing. Two years afterwards the young Rajah was poisoned by his Omras, and Maun Sing was restored to the throne. We now resume the thread of our original narrative.

While a civil war was raging in Marwar, the north-western frontier of the Bahawalpur territory was disturbed by the hostile movements of Runjeet Sing, the Sikh chief, against Multan. On the 2nd of Mohurrum, 1222 (A. D. 1807), the intelligence of his march from Lahore was received in the Khan's court. It was followed by a deputation from the Multan governor, who urged the necessity of a ready assistance against his formidable enemy. The deputation was kindly received, and dismissed with a satisfactory answer. Azeem Khan, Seifullah Khan, Dost Mohammed, and some other Daoodputras, were soon afterwards sent towards Multan, to assist Muzuffir Khan in the threatened attack.

The Khan, meanwhile, took measures to reconcile the

Sikh chief, by sending him, through his own secretary, Dhunput Rae, a horse and a camel with silver trappings, besides eleven Parchos, or pieces of silk. The Munshee obtained a ready and attentive audience, during which a long conversation passed on various subjects, and among others about Multan, and the bravery of its Afghans, of which he gave an interesting account.

Runjeet Sing, on his arrival at Multan, at once laid siege to the fort, and allowed the country in the vicinity to be ravaged and wasted by his Sikhs. Numbers of the subjects, owing to these outrages, were obliged to take shelter in the Bahawalpur territory, during which time they were provided with the necessary provisions at the Khan's own expense.

After the siege had been carried on for some time, Runjeet Sing demanded the delivery of the fort of Multan, on condition that the rest of the territory should be allowed to continue in the possession of Muzuffir Khan. The latter consulted the Khan on the subject, through his agent, Mahsen Shah, when, after a deliberate consideration, Bahawal Khan advised him to hold the place, and to disregard the proposition made by the Sikh chieftain. He also said that he himself was united with him in this measure; and, accordingly, made some overtures on the subject to Runjeet through his agent.

As the siege continued much longer than was expected, the Sikh chief, despairing of successs, broke up the campaign, and returned to Lahore. Before his highness retired, he sent some presents, consisting of an elephant and a shawl, through the agency of Fakeer Azeez-ud-Deen, his Persian secretary. The Fakeer, among other friendly assurances, informed the Khan that his master had given up the siege of Multan solely from a regard to himself. On his dismissal, he was presented with a purse of a thousand rupees.

As the Khan was engaged about this time in a shooting excursion on the banks of the Sutlej, he met with an accident by a fall from his horse, which slightly injured him in the leg.

Soon after the departure of Azeez-ud-Deen, the Khan was visited by his brother, Amam-ud-Deen, who came with some further friendly messages on the part of Runjeet Sing.

Muzuffir Khan, being disposed to proceed on a pilgrimage to Mecca, invested his elder son, Surfaraz Khan, with his government, which measure was also confirmed by the nominal king at the time in Cabul. The Nawab next consulted the Khan about his intended journey; when he was told in reply, that if he considered his territory safe, his design was most praiseworthy.

A party of the commissariat department in the Khan's service, which had proceeded to make the necessary purchases of grain in the direction of Ponkel and Bikaner, was interrupted on its way at Deenghur by Dilawer Khan, the son of Khoda Buksh Marufanee. Some of them were put to the sword, and their property plundered. The Khan was much displeased at his insolent demeanour; and to punish him, sent a detachment under the command of Azmet Khan Daoodputra, who wrested the fortress from the hands of the Marufanee chief, and removed his family to Majghur.

Khoda Buksh, being anxious to recover his fort,

applied for aid to his old friend the chief of Bikaner, who sent him fifty Sawars on the occasion. To destroy him was therefore considered of great importance; and hence the Khan was induced to send a large force, commanded by Nasir Khan, to attack and occupy Majghur. On his arrival, he immediately laid siege to the place; upon which Khoda Buksh feeling his inability to hold out, was obliged to surrender himself. The place was accordingly garrisoned by the Daoodputra troops, while Khoda Buksh was conducted to the presence of the Khan, who ordered him to be confined in the village of Keerhalee, within twelve koss to the west of Bahawalpur.

The seizure of Khoda Buksh was followed by the punishment of Jawal Khan Arbanee, and Mohammed Khan Jawanee, who assisted him in his insurrection.

Kaempur and Jawalpur, as well as other places held by them in Jaghir, were forthwith confiscated and included in the Khalsa lands. Mohammed Khan, in consequence, went over to Multan, with a view of inducing Muzuffir Khan to intercede in his behalf.

It has been already stated, that the Nawab was making preparations to proceed to Mecca. His arrangements being now complete, he set out on his journey, accompanied by his protegé. On entering the Bahawalpur territory, he was received and treated hospitably; and on his arrival at the village of Manjeewala, near Uch, the Khan proceeded in person by water, with a party of 500 Sawars, to visit the Nawab. They had a long conference on various subjects; and towards the breaking up of the meeting, the Nawab interceded in behalf of his guest, and placing his hand in that of the Khan, obtained his pardon; after which, Bahawal retired to his own tent. The next day, the Khan presented the Nawab with five boats, including one with a room for his own personal use, besides some trifling presents in cash and clothes to his companions. The Nawab, being thus furnished with boats, at once proceeded on his journey by water.

The considerate attention shown by the Khan to the governor of Multan made a favourable impression on the amiable disposition of his son, Surfaraz Khan. To return the compliment, he leased Khanpur to the Daoodputra chief, together with three other districts.

Fourteen months afterwards, intelligence was brought of Muzuffir Khan's return from Mecca; and that in his progress through Sindh, he had met with a kind reception on the part of the Meers. Orders were immediately issued for a similar reception in the Bahawalpur territory; and on his arrival at the village of Noorwala, the Khan again proceeded to visit the Nawab. The conversation was chiefly on topics regarding Arabia.

In the evening of the same day, the Nawab quite unexpectedly returned the visit of the Khan, and with him concerted some measures against the Sikhs. They both continued in this place for three days, when they parted, one going to Multan and the other to his own capital.

The next season was commenced by sending a friendly embassy to the Meers of Talpur, which further strengthened the cordial relations between the two courts.

Peace was soon afterwards again disturbed by the insurrection of Khoda Buksh and Ismael Khan, the sons of Subzul Khan Daoodputra. The Khan was, therefore, obliged to despatch a force to put them down; and on coming into collision with them, a severe fight occurred, when the rebels were compelled to fly. They were, however, overtaken by their pursuers, and Khoda Buksh was taken prisoner. The whole Ilaka held in Jaghir by the insurgent chiefs fell into the hands of the victors, when the towns of Ahmedpur, Lumma, Mohammedpur and Kot-Subzul, as well as Pehlagee, were occupied and garrisoned by the Khan's own troops.

His son, Fatteh Ali, and Ismael Khan fled to Sindh, and afterwards threw themselves on the protection of Sohrab Khan of Kheirpur, when Fatteh Ali delivered a written engagement to the latter, by which he made over to him his hereditary right to his father's territory, which had been wrested from him by Bahawal Khan. The Meer communicated the subject to Gholam Ali, the ruler of Hyderabad, who readily approved of the negotiations, and forthwith ordered an army of 30,000 horse and foot to be employed in the recovery of the transferred territory. On their arrival in the neighbourhood of Subzul-Kot, they succeeded in taking possession of a place named Beng-Bahara; but their further progress was checked by the timely arrival of the Daoodputra troops under the command of Nasir Khan Korkeich and Soona Khan of the Kheiree tribe. Indeed, Sohrab Khan, who commanded the Sindh army in person, was so much convinced of the superiority of his opponents, that he did not even consider it safe to continue in the field, but instantly withdrew himself within his own territory without coming to a battle. The Bahawalpur troops, therefore, also retraced their steps to their own capital.

This untoward retreat of the Sindh army was perhaps

occasioned by the intelligence which was received of the approach of Shah Shuja, who was on his march against Sindh. But their minds were soon rendered easy on the subject by the proclamation of Prince Keiser, the son of Shah Zaman, at Cabul, to the exclusion of his uncle Shuja. He was set on the throne by Shir Mohammed Khan and Meer Waez, who were men of considerable influence in the Khorasan court. As soon as the Prince was placed on the throne, orders were issued to the Ameers of Sindh, as well as to Bahawal Khan and the Governor of Multan, directing them to seize Shah Shuja. The Khan in consequence posted guards on the ferries of the Indus and Chenab to prevent the passage of his majesty, and an army was likewise prepared by the Sindh chiefs to oppose his entrance into their own territory. The Shah, however, reconciled the Sindhians by making some overtures of cordiality through Mohammed Khan Berohee, and he was therefore allowed to pass unmolested to Methan-Kot, and from thence to Dereh Ghazi Khan.

Here Shah Shuja was deserted by Vizir Fatteh Khan and Mohammed Khan, who went over to Candahar. Distracted in mind by the defection of his own people, the Shah continued his march to Peshawur; but, soon after his arrival, Shahzada Keiser came down from Cabul with a large force, and the Shah was therefore obliged to meet him in the field, when an action took place, which terminated in the total defeat of Keiser. The Mukhtar-ud-Doula (Shir Mohammed Khan) was slain in the midst of the battle, and his protegé, the defeated prince, was therefore obliged to throw himself on the mercy of the Shah, when he was generously pardoned for his past conduct.

After this victory, Shah Shuja returned to Cabul, where he seized and put to death Meer Waez, the other ringleader.

About this period, further additions were made to the Bahawalpur territory. The fort of Islamghur, situated in the Cholistan, had originally belonged to Jeyselmeer, but had been subsequently seized by the late Hajji Khan. On the fall of Gurhee, his chief town, and his imprisonment, his son Abdullah still held out in Islamghur, and bade defiance to the Khan's authority.

The suppression of this rebel attracted the early notice of Bahawal Khan; and with this intention he consulted Moolraj, the chief of Jeyselmeer, who promised that he would help him in forwarding his political views. But the voluntary surrender of Abdullah prevented the employment of force in that quarter; and, to reward the young man for his ready submission, the Khan restored him to his hereditary possession of Gurhee, with with its dependencies, while a governor was appointed directly from the court to take charge of the evacuated fortress.

The peaceful occupation of Gurhee nevertheless excited the jealousy of the chief of Jeyselmeer, who therefore, regardless of the existing friendship, induced Fazul Ali to sell the fort of Deenghur for 40,000 rupees, when he gave it the name of Kishunghur. No sooner was the intelligence of this transaction brought to the Khan, than he despatched a large force to punish Fazul Ali for his treacherous conduct. They soon succeeded in depriving him of all his fortifications and lands, and obliged him to appear in person before the Khan to entreat for pardon, which was willingly granted, while a suitable provision was also made for him by the assignment of a separate Jaghir.

Intelligence was brought that the Mukdoom Sahib of Uch, an inveterate enemy of the Khan, had died at Kaderpur, in Sindh, and was succeeded in his office of priesthood and in his territorial property by his son Abbas Ali, who after this time assumed the title of Mukdoom Shums-ud-Deen. Mohammed Ghow, his other son, also declared himself his successor at Uch, and was recognised by the Khan, who proceeded in person to that place, and performed the customary ceremony of placing on his head the "Turban of Recognition."

FROM THE ARRIVAL OF A BRITISH DEPUTATION TO THE DEATH OF BAHAWAL KHAN II.

Before we enter on the narrative of the passage of an embassy from the British Government to the Court of Khorasan, it is necessary we should give a brief account of the English nation and their country, so that the reader may have a clearer understanding of the matters we are about to relate.

England (Great Britain) is one of the islands of Europe, extending 600 miles in length and 400 in breadth. London is its metropolis, the circumference of which is twenty-four English miles; so that, without exaggeration in point of extent, dimensions or beauty, it cannot be surpassed by any of the towns of India, Persia, Turan, etc. Within ten koss, its suburbs are also said to be covered with delightful gardens and noble buildings, skilfully constructed and arranged, affording ample accommodation to inhabitants and travellers. It is a fixed rule with every citizen, rich or poor, young or old, to whitewash his dwelling once a year, so that all the buildings are as brilliant as a mirror. Hence the town, with its streets and houses, is always kept in clean order, which presents a lively and pleasant view to a visitor. Its streets and lanes are broad, and its roads are paved with stones of various colours, whilst the shops are very beautiful and plentifully supplied with articles of various and attractive kinds. The streets are so brilliantly illuminated at night that they forcibly remind you of the "Joshun of Fareidoon;" besides the lights with which each shop is furnished, the streets and houses are lined every night with Kandeils or lanterns hanging from iron poles, which are furnished at the public expense, and which is a matter of great congratulation to the inhabitants, who enjoy this most wonderful and interesting sight every night without intermission. The illumination of the town continues throughout the night, commencing with the setting and continuing to the rising of the sun. London contains twenty lakhs of inhabitants.

To England are added the islands of Scotland and Ireland; and these three united go by the name of Great Britain. The English are surpassed by no nation in science and art. They are the best astronomers, geometricians, mathematicians and musicians; and also are perfect masters of natural philosophy. Their manufacture of cotton cloths, cutlery, watches, as well as their knowledge of casting metals and other arts, are without comparison and beyond description.

The House of Commons consists of about 660 representatives of the towns and shires of the kingdom. They debate on matters touching the political, judicial and revenue affairs; and also make laws for the guidance of the government of the country. When any new measure has passed the House of Commons, it is next discussed in the Upper House, or House of Lords, which consists of nearly 300 Omras or Peers of the Realm. If it meets with the approbation of the House of Lords after due deliberation, it is submitted to the Privy Council, consisting of thirty nobles of the country, chosen by the sovereign to advise him in the affairs of the state.

The members of the House of Commons are elected by the gentry of the towns and districts, each enjoying an annual income of not less than fifty rupees, as their representatives to watch over their interests. They are generally men of great experience in the business of the state, both political and judicial, and of high talents and abilities in point of learning.

By the Court of Directors is meant the East India Company, which consists of twenty-four individuals. They lease from the king's government the East India possessions; and the entire management of them is, therefore, entrusted to their care. If they are disposed to introduce any new law, or wish to carry out any political measure of great importance, they are under the obligation of previously obtaining the assent of the three legislative powers. If the proposition is approved of, their consent is communicated to the Court of Directors through the Board of Control, consisting of six gentlemen selected by the king's government to watch over the affairs of India.

The annual income of Great Britain amounts to fifty crores of rupees. There are seven different coins, which are known by separate names, in circulation in that country. In the idiom of the English language, a Crown is equal to two rupees; a half Crown is equal to one rupee, and a Shilling to half a rupee. A Sovereign is a gold coin, valued at eleven rupees; and a Half-Sovereign, at five and a half rupees.

The army consists of 106,000 men, viz. ninety-six regiments of infantry, thirty of cavalry, and 10,000 artillerymen. Besides these, they have a militia, which amounts to 200,000. They are furnished with arms by government, and concentrated once in the year for two months, when they are taught the military tactics.

The attendance of the British ambassador at the court of Persia, has been chiefly for the purpose of preventing the descent of the Russians on India. With that view, Fatteh Ali Shah, the king of that country, has blocked up the Pass of the Zulmat mountains, by fixing the seat of his government in Turan. Failing in their object in the court of Persia, the Russian Government opened suitable overtures with the court of Turan. At this time, the alarm of the invasion of India meditated by France through the way of Yarkand and Samarkand becoming prevalent, the British Government determined to send an embassy to the court of Khorasan, to establish friendly relations between the two governments, and thereby to thwart the aggressive views of Russia.

At the same time, the growing power of Runjeet Sing in the Punjab, made it necessary to include his court also in the treaty of amity and friendship. Mr. C. T. Metcalfe (late Lord Metcalfe), an officer of extensive experience, was therefore selected on the occasion by the British Government to negotiate with the Sikh chief; and accordingly he joined the Sikh camp from Calcutta, and communicated to Runjeet Sing the object of his mission at Amritsar. The negotiations were purposely delayed by the Punjab ruler for some time; but an event occurred which expedited an amicable conclusion.

The Mohurrum, when the Mussulmans of India celebrate the martyrdom of Husain by making Tazias, commenced while Mr. Metcalfe was encamped at Amritsar, the religious place of the Sikhs, and the Mohammedans of his escort began to celebrate the death of the saint as usual. The Akalees, a fanatic sect of the Sikhs, taking umbrage at this circumstance, attacked the camp of the envoy; but the escort, though composed of a small body of men, boldly opposed and repulsed them. Runjeet Sing himself came up at the time, and made a suitable apology to the envoy; and at the same time was much struck with the bravery of this small body of British troops. Subsequently the pending negotiations were brought to a satisfactory termination, and the envoy returned to the British frontier.

In the mean time, the Sikh chiefs between the Sutlej and the Jumna, being alarmed at the all-absorbing power of Runjeet Sing, had entreated of the British Government to take them under its protection. A deputation, composed of Bhaee Lal Sing of Kuthul, Bhag Sing, and Sahib Sing of Jeind, Jeswunt Sing of Nabha, and the chief of Petyala, accordingly opened communications on the subject with the British authorities. Their solicitation was complied with; and in concert with them, a Chawnee, or cantonment, of British troops was established at Loodianah.

When the intelligence of the termination of the foregoing negotiations was received by the authorities in England, they gave orders to expedite the despatch of the deputation to Khorasan by Bikaner and Bahawalpur, etc. As the passage of the embassy through the sandy desert of Marwar was supposed to be rather difficult without the assistance of the Bahawalpur chief, Mr. Seton, the resident at Delhi, was directed by the Governor-General of India to secure the good offices of the Khan. The resident, accordingly, deputed Meer Izzet Ullah Khan, a respectable native of Delhi, with a letter to the Bahawalpur court. The Meer waited on the Khan at Deirawer, and communicated to him the object of his mission. The Khan held a consultation on the occasion with the nobles of his court; and although some of them were against the passage of the British mission through the Bahawalpur territory, yet the Khan, from friendly motives, readily gave his consent. The agent was therefore dismissed with a Khelat, and a reply to the resident, assuring him of a full concurrence in his views; and the Meer returned to Delhi.

Upon this, the Honourable Mr. Elphinstone and Mr. Strachey, who was well known for his high merits and for the favour which he enjoyed with Fatteh Ali Shah, the Persian Monarch, together with twelve other officers, were selected to proceed on this mission to the court of Khorasan. The deputation accordingly started, and by regular marches arrived at Bikaner, where it halted for four days. The chief of that place, Surat Sing, treated it with marked respect and hospitality; and to assure the envoy of his friendship, went so far as to lay the key of the fort of Bikaner before that officer; but it was returned to him with suitable acknowledgments regarding his friendly feelings. Surat Sing also took an opportunity to complain in detail against the Khan of Bahawalpur.

After this short repose, the deputation renewed its progress, when the Khan sent out numbers of camels laden with supplies of every available sort of provision, as well as spices of all sorts for its use; and at the same time addressed a complimentary letter to the envoy.

At length, by the assistance of guides, the mission reached Majghur, the extreme frontier part of Bahawalpur, in the Cholistan, where its arrival was most cordially welcomed by Azmet Khan, the officer who was deputed to wait on and to attend to the wants of the deputation.

They made another halt of three days at this place, and on the fourth day continued their progress to the capital. When within two marches, the envoy was again met by another deputation on the part of the Khan. Bahawal Khan, who was absent at Deirawer, also moved to Bahawalpur, and erected a pavilion supplied with carpets, on the bank of the river, for the reception of the mission, whose arrival was greeted with due honours by a third deputation, composed of the nobles of the Khan's court.

A Zeyafet, consisting of all the luxuries, liquors and fruits included, was sent to the envoy, and numbers of dishes of Pilow, Motanjow, Kabobs, etc. etc. etc., were at the same time provided for the use of the party. The Khan, moreover, issued a general order, by the beat of Tom-tom, prohibiting the shopkeepers of the town from asking any price for the articles which they sold to any persons belonging to the mission, as they were to be fully paid for by the government.

In the afternoon, the Khan paid a visit to the envoy in his tent, when he was met by the latter at the end of the carpet. The meeting lasted for some hours, during which the conference turned on various friendly topics.

The following day, Mr. Strachey, with three other officers, waited on the Khan, and was welcomed by the latter in person, at the Lube-fursh, or end of the carpet, and seated immediately beside him. On entering the Durbar the gentlemen took off their hats. As the officer was well versed in the Asiatic manners and idioms, the conversation was very interesting and pleasing to both parties. It was chiefly regarding Shiraz, Ispahan, Teheran, and the numerous offspring of Fatteh Ali Shah, of Persia. This cheerful meeting continued till sunset, when the gentlemen took leave and retired to their camp. On their dismissal, they were presented with two good horses, and two Sandnee, or riding camels, with silver trappings.

On the following morning, the Khan's visit was returned by the envoy, accompanied by thirteen other officers of the mission, who came in palanquins; and, on entering the Durbar took off their hats. The envoy was seated on the same Musnud with the Khan. The visit lasted nearly three hours; and the subjects of conversation were about England and its kings, Rome, Constantinople, India and Persia, etc. The envoy afterwards took leave and returned to his camp, whither he was followed by fourteen trays of clothes of various kinds, with fourteen horses with gold and silver trappings, whioh were presented by the Khan to the gentlemen of the mission.

On the fifth day, the Khan again returned the visit, accompanied by Gossaeen Behar Rae, Nasir Khan the commander-in-chief, Munshee Salamut Rae, while Doulut Rae stood behind his master with the Taoosee-Bad-Kush or fan. In the course of the conference, the Khan observed to the envoy, that the tract of land which he held was the gift of Almighty God; but that Runjeet Sing, owing to the decline of the Khorasan monarchy, was ill-disposed towards him; and that his ill-will would be still further increased on hearing of the friendship which was now so happily established between him and the British Government. In reply, the Khan was assured by the envoy, that his enemy would be considered that of the British Government.

A friendly treaty was afterwards drawn up, signed and sealed by the envoy and Mr. Strachey, and was delivered to Bahawal Khan. The Khan's attentions were now further increased towards the mission. He sent a nobleman almost every day to make the customary inquiries after the health of the gentlemen.

On the seventh day, the envoy again went over to see Bahawal Khan, by whom he was received with every possible civility and honour. He announced his intention of renewing his march to Peshawar by way of Multan. Although the Khan entreated him to remain for a few days longer, he nevertheless urged the point on the plea of necessity, and accordingly took his final leave and returned to the camp. As he was leaving the Durbar, the Khan assured him that his territory was considered to be as the "Sahiban's" own country. To facilitate the departure of the mission, the Khan furnished the envoy with sixty camels for his use.

After two days, when the mission was ready to depart,

the Khan paid a farewell visit, when an interchange of presents took place on either side. The Khan presented the envoy with some trays of cloths manufactured in his own territory, and with a sum of 14,000 rupees in cash; whilst the presents sent to him in return by the Envoy, consisted of two telescopes, one carbine, one gun, two pistols, two matchlocks, one palanquin, one elephant, and one pedometer, besides a few knives and scissors. The Khan distributed among the bearers of the presents 1,200 rupees.

The following morning, being the 10th of Shawal, 1222, A. H., the mission crossed over the Sutlej and encamped on the right bank; while the Khan proceeded on a shooting excursion to the desert of Adam Dhen. He also crossed the river, and succeeded in shooting a great deal of game, some of which he sent to the envoy. The Khan's servant, who was sent in charge of the Shikar or game, was presented on this occasion with 300 rupees by the envoy; but the servant fell unde the displeasure of his master for having accepted the present.

On its arrival at Multan, the mission was honourably received and hospitably treated by Surfaraz Khan, whose father, Muzuffir Khan, was absent on pilgrimage; but the envoy was somewhat annoyed at the conduct of some of the Afghan servants who entered his tent with shoes on. In short, the mission at length reached Peshawar, where they met Shah Shuja.

The next day the envoy waited on the king, and explained to him the object of his deputation, assuring him, at the same time, that the British Government already held the extensive country of Hindustan, and aspired to no additional territorial acquisitions; and that the only object of the mission to his court was to establish a mutual and cordial friendship between the two governments. The king was highly pleased at the overtures of the envoy, and addressed a letter to his Britannic majesty, accepting of the friendly terms proposed by the envoy. Pending a reply, the mission was detained at his court. Soon afterwards, the king proposed to give the fort of Atok in Jaghir to the Sahiban; but this predilection chagrined the Durranee nobles of his court to such a degree, that they came to a unanimous resolution to attack the camp of the mission; and had it not been for the timely protection of Feizullah Khan, a chief of great power, they would have executed their design without any scruple. The mission, in consequence, took the earliest opportunity to make its retreat unobserved across the Atok, on its way to Delhi; and the Shah, being quite unable to control its proceedings, could only express his great regret at its conduct.

The Khan had been labouring for a long time past under a weakness in the stomach, and want of digestion, as well as the swelling of his belly. When he visited Muzuffir Khan on his return from Mecca, the latter gave him the copy of a receipt prescribed by his physician, Abud-Deen; but even the use of this gave him no relief. On the 17th Jamaddussanee, as the Khan got up from a Kehloola, or the afternoon nap, to appease the inflammation of the stomach and liver, he applied a plaster consisting of various ingredients. This process brought on insensibility; but on recovery, it was followed by excruciating pains in his kidneys. He continued suffering from this disease for five days, when he was partly relieved of the pains by the wise prescription of Ahsunullah, his physician. On the first of Rajab, however, he had a relapse, and appeared to be labouring under great weakness. After midnight he came again to his senses, upon which he was left by the physician. During the night he got up to make water, when faintness returned, and he laid his head down on a pillow. The physician immediately attended him again, and felt his pulse, when he found that death was approaching; and, in fact, he only survived one or two Hindustanee Ghurrees, when he surrendered his soul to his Maker.

Mobarik Khan, his elder son, as has been already stated, was in confinement. His second and favourite son was therefore unanimously raised to the vacant throne by the nobles in the fort of Deirawer, where the Khan died. After the usual ceremonies of installation, the rites of burial were performed. The proclaimed heir was attended by almost every member of the family, as well as by the nobility, etc.; and the remains of the late chief were buried in the royal cemetery outside the fort, seven hundred paces to the east of it.

The late Khan left a treasury full of money and jewels, besides a considerable number of horses, camels, and clothes of various kinds, as well as valuable carpets, tents, and vessels for domestic purposes, and a good armoury and library. The army was also left in admirable condition, with a hundred and fifteen pieces of ordnance of various calibre. He built twenty-one fortresses in the

Cholistan; and left seven virtuous sons, namely, first, Mobarik, who continued a prisoner until his death; second, Sadik Khan, who succeeded the late chief; besides Feizullah, Khodayar, Hajji, Nasir, and Kader Bukhsh.

MOHAMMED SADIK KHAN II.

On the death of his father, Sadik Khan ascended the vacant throne without the least opposition. The Daoodputra chiefs and the state officers readily tendered their allegiance, by offering him the customary presents, and receiving the usual Khelats. Letters of condolence on the death of his honoured parent, and of congratulation on his own accession, were likewise received from the neighbouring princes: in short, everything combined to smile upon his peaceful accession.

A new ministry was afterwards formed, without causing any excitement. The privy seal was entrusted to the custody of Mulram Munshee, a man of high character; the office of premier was conferred on Nasir Khan Beloochee, of the Korkeich tribe; that of commander-in-chief on Fatteh Mohammed Ghoree; and of Bukhshee, or paymaster of the troops, on Mohammed Yakoob; while Mukbool Mohammed and Noor Mohammed were raised to the office of general accountants. Molwee Maeen-ud-Deen was appointed chief justice, and Molwee Shir Ali to the office of preceptor to the children of the Khan. Ghaus Buksh, Gossaeen Behar Shah, Sultan Ahmed Shah, and Nawab Fukr-ud-Deen, were selected as chief advisers and councillors.

Notwithstanding the formation of the new government, and his unopposed accession, the Khan did not consider his authority secure, as long as the rightful heir, his elder brother Mobarik, continued alive. To get rid of this unfortunate prince was therefore to him an object of the first consideration; and in his prime minister he found a willing tool to relieve him from this anxiety. This ruthless officer, wishing to convince his inhuman master of his service and loyal attachment, forthwith deputed one of his relatives, named Osman, on this service, to the fortress of Ramkolee, to which place the prince had been subsequently removed from Deirawer. The innocent Mobarik was taken out from the dungeon and removed to the Cholistan, where he was inhumanly assassinated in cold blood, and buried under a sand-hill. Having been thus relieved of his rightful rival, the Khan next wished to remove the stigma which this barbarous act attached to his character. With this view, he threw the blame of the horrid deed on his minister, and ordered the assassin, Osman, to be hanged, to atone for the blood of his innocent brother. But his subsequent conduct towards Nasir Khan proved that this was merely a pretence; for the minister daily increased in favour, and was distinguished by the grant of Khelats. His own brother, Deen Mohammed, was also soon afterwards appointed to the office of governor of the fort of Deirawer.

No sooner had Sadik Mohammed completed his arrangements for the internal administration of his government, than he quitted Deirawer, and proceeded into the country to receive further proofs of allegiance from his vassals and subjects. On his arrival at Ahmedpur, he was waited on by agents on the part of the rulers of Multan and Jeyselmeer, and of the Derehs Ismael Khan and Ghazi Khan, etc., who brought the customary presents in celebration of his accession, and were dismissed with corresponding etiquette. A public Durbar was likewise held, at which the rest of the Daoodputra chiefs and Jaghirdars who had not yet made their obeisance, attended and publicly acknowledged the authority of their new chief.

After these ceremonies, the Khan returned to the fort of Deirawer. The peace of his territory, however, was not of long duration, but was soon disturbed by a foreign foe. Meer Sohrab Khan, of Kheirpur, in Sindh, having been invited by the Beloochees of the Mozaree tribe, took possession of the fort of Omerkot, and began to lay waste the other part of the Daoodputra territory in that quarter. Troops were in consequence immediately despatched under the commander-in-chief to suppress these incursions. The minister was also sent in the same direction, to collect the militia of the country, and to send them across the Indus, to join the troops sent in advance. The Mozarees could not withstand this overwhelming force, and were dispersed without the occurrence of much bloodshed; while the places which had been occupied by them were easily recovered, and re-garrisoned by the Daoodputra troops. As soon as the news of the expulsion of the foreign invaders was announced in the court, a royal salute was fired in honour of the event; and the officers who had made themselves prominent by their valour in this war, were distinguished by marked favour,—by the testimonial of Khelats, and by other suitable presents.

The joy arising from this success was enhanced at the same time by the arrival of a firman from his majesty Shah Shuja-ul-Mulk, confirming the succession of Mohammed Sadik.

The late expulsion which the Meer of Kheirpur had experienced, instead of damping his warlike spirit, served to stimulate him still further. As soon as the Khan's troops had retired, he renewed his incursions, with a view of re-occupying the Subzul-Kot. Immediately on the receipt of this intelligence, troops were again sent to that quarter, under the command of the minister and the commander-in-chief, to defend the fort; but Sohrab Khan, having received a reinforcement of five thousand horse and foot from Gholam Ali, the chief of Hyderabad, was found to have become more formidable than he had been at any previous time. This intelligence alarmed the Khan; and after the Eid of Ramzan, he proceeded in person to Ahmedpur, whence he sent out a deputation, consisting of the Syeds and Mullahs, or learned men, to persuade the enemy to withdraw, as he had never given him any offence. The mission, however, failed in its object, and recourse was at length had to arms. A battle accordingly ensued, in which, notwithstanding the superiority of number, the enemy were unsuccessful. They were obliged to sue for the cessation of hostilities; but entreated, that as their retreat might be attributed to defeat, one of the sons of the Khan might accompany them to Hyderabad. They also affirmed that this course would cause the re-establishment of friendly relations between the two states. The Khan, who was not indisposed to the restoration of tranquillity and order in his territory, acceded to their request, and Roheem Yar Khan, the eldest son of Sadik, and the future Bahawal Khan the Third, was accordingly selected on the occasion. The young Khan in consequence proceeded with the Sindhians, first to Kheirpur, where he was properly and considerately received by Sohrab Khan; and thence to Hyderabad. On his attending the Durbar, Meer Gholam Ali, the chief, seated him on the same Musnud with himself. He was accommodated in a comfortable building in the town, and was treated very hospitably.

The Khan, after the withdrawal of the Sindhian troops, returned to Deirawer on the 12th of Zugad, in the same year. Soon after his arrival, he received a letter from Mohammed Shah, who, on the expulsion of Shah Shuja, had occupied the throne of the Khorasan kingdom. The royal mandate was at the same time accompanied with a letter from Vizir Fatteh Khan. The Khan placed the mandate on his head, and evinced every other proof of his allegiance to the new monarch. A royal salute was fired in honour of the event; and the town was illuminated at night, to display the Khan's loyalty. After these ceremonies were over, the Khan next shewed his marked sense of the duty of such of his officers as had distinguished themselves in the late war, by the grant of valuable presents.

In the same year, Gholam Rasool, the Sijadeh-Nasheen, or occupant of the carpet of the famous religious saint, Shaker Fareid of Patan, having died a natural death, the Khan, according to custom, addressed a letter of condolence to his successor, and sent it with the usual clothes presented on such occasions.*

* It is customary in India to present a turban and a pair of shawls on the occasion of a new successor or heir. The custom prevails throughout the country, and is observed by a chief towards his dependants, or by the latter towards the former, on similar occasions.

Nawab Jubbar Khan, the step-brother of Fatteh Khan, having been nominated to the office of the governor of Dereh Ghazi Khan, the new ruler arrived in that place, and took peaceful possession of his charge.

The Khan afterwards set out on a hunting excursion across the Sutlej, and after some time returned to Bahawalpur, where, in order to gain the good opinion of the religious people, he visited an assembly of the Mullahs collected on the occasion in the grand mosque, and attended a sermon preached by the famous preacher Abudeen. From Bahawalpur, the Khan proceeded on a tour to the Cholistan, or Sandy Desert, to examine the condition of his fortresses situated in that quarter. He was absent on this journey till the grand Eid, when he returned to Deirawer to celebrate that festival.

A knowledge of the passing events of Lahore having become necessary, the Khan in the same month deputed a news-writer to Runjeet's court, with directions to keep him informed of the state of affairs in that quarter.

His highness soon after attended at the marriage of his minister, at his village Taroda. The nuptials were celebrated with great pomp, and rich presents were offered to his royal highness by Nasir Khan on the occasion, while the former, as usual, made him a marriage-present in money.

Gossaeen Beharjee being a man of great talent and merit, rose higher in the confidence of his master than in the esteem of his colleagues. His rising influence, therefore, excited the jealousy of the latter; and as the Gossaeen had lately built a magnificent Hindu temple in the town of Bahawalpur, this building furnished his enemies with a plausible ground for accusing him to the Nawab. They charged him with having disgraced Islamism by providing means of idolatry for the Hindus. The temple was demolished, and was followed by the decline of its founder's credit at court.

Intelligence was received about this period of the utter overthrow of Shah Shuja, and his arrival at Lahore, where Runjeet Sing took advantage of the distressed condition of his guest, to deprive him of the famous Kohinoor.

A conspiracy, which was formed for the assassination of the Khan, was fortunately discovered before the conspirators had matured their plans. Khodayar Khan, his own brother, together with some other members of the family, was at the head of it. The traitors were, however, betrayed by a Kidmutghar, or attendant, named Moosa, who disclosed the secret to the Khan. Khodayar, and Yoonis, one of his attendants, who was the chief supporter of the projected plot, were forthwith apprehended. The former was thrown into a dungeon, while the latter was immediately executed.

The arrival of Shah Shuja in the Punjaub had occasioned an alarm in the court of the usurper of his throne; and to prevent any revival of the Khan's old attachment towards his enemy, Mohammed Shah deputed an agent to Bahawalpur, with a valuable Khelat and a letter from the Vizir Fatteh Khan, in order to gain the Khan over to his cause. The envoy, named Munsoor Khan Durranee, was received with great consideration, and treated very hospitably during his stay in the Bahawalpur court. He was followed by a letter from the king in his own handwriting. These persuasive measures succeeded in inducing the Khan to remain neutral in the civil wars for the throne of Khorasan.

Muzuffir Khan, the governor of Multan, was, however, still favourably disposed towards the ex-king. This circumstance induced the latter to endeavour to obtain admission and refuge for his Harem at Multan, but without effect.

In the meantime, the public attention was engaged by the sudden appearance of Runjeet Sing on the other bank of the Sutlej opposite to Uch. On the pretext of a certain demand from Muzuffir Khan, Runjeet Sing laid siege to the fort of Multan on the 20th of February, 1810; and Muzuffir Khan made every possible arrangement for a bold defence. The first thing he did was to remove his family, under the care of some of his trustworthy officers, to Uch, across the river, which they reached safely, and were properly treated and protected by the Mukdoom Sahib, the possessor of the place. Runjeet Sing entertained some fear of a diversion being made in favour of the besieged on the part of Bahawalpur, and with this idea he deputed an agent to the Khan to temporise with him should he have any such design. He moreover asked him to send him a reinforcement of troops. Sadik Khan did not think it proper to give a direct refusal to the Sikh chiefs; and, apparently complying with his request, despatched 500 Sawars across the river, but with instructions to guard the fords rather than to succour the Sikhs.

Runjeet's anxiety as to any reinforcement from Bahawalpur being relieved, he proceeded to prosecute the siege with the greatest ardour. A mine having been run under the walls of the fort, was ready for explosion; but being at the same time countermined by another from the fort, it was suddenly blown up. By this accident, the Sikhs suffered the loss of many valuable men, particularly of Ater Sing, one of the principal officers of Runjeet Sing's army. Irritated by this, he ordered the whole of his artillery to open fire on the fort, but still without making any impression. On the 21st of March, Runjeet ordered a general assault; but the Sikhs were repulsed with great loss. All these reverses served to dishearten the Sikhs and to encourage the defenders. Besides this, no impression had hitherto been made on the walls; and the supplies, notwithstanding every arrangement to secure their safe conveyance from Lahore, both by land and water, had become very scarce. The Atta at this time was selling at two seers for the rupee. In spite of these difficulties, Runjeet Sing continued resolute; and, on the 25th instant, he ordered a more vigorous assault than before, but still without effect, as he again suffered a loss of forty men. On the 29th, however, the Sikhs succeeded in making a breach; but it was forthwith repaired by the Afghans. The Sikhs next dug another mine, but apparently with as little skill and caution as the preceding one; for it was again countermined by the besieged. It so happened, that when the mine was announced to be ready, Runjeet ordered the Sirdars, Hira Sing Nulwa, Mush Sing and Setij Sing, to make an examination. While these officers were in the mine, the Afghans exploded the counter-mine and killed Setij Sing with forty men; but his two companions had the good fortune to escape, being only slightly burnt in the face. The siege, however, was still protracted till the middle of April, when Runjeet, finding all his endeavours vain, had recourse to a stratagem. He forged a letter, on the part of Shah Shuja, in the name of his agent, Habibulla Khan, who was in attendance on him in the camp, demanding the delivery of the fort to Runjeet for the admission into it of his family, as Muzuffir Khan was bound to do by his engagement. The letter was sent to Muzuffir, but was not obeyed; and Runjeet Sing, being tired of the prolonged operations, and still finding the fort impregnable, was at last compelled to grant terms, and retired to Lahore on the 25th of April, on receiving the sum of one lakh and eighty thousand rupees for war-expenses.

The Khan of Bahawalpur, though urgently entreated by Muzuffir Khan, neglected to send him any succour, probably in order to remain on good terms with the Sikhs. When he was invited by Nawab Jubbar Khan, the governor of Dereh Ghazi Khan, and the chief of Dereh Ismael Khan, to support the distressed Nawab, he expressed his willingness to co-operate with him, but never seriously set about it. He, however, treated Muzuffir's family during their stay in his territory with politeness and hospitality; and to encourage them, he sent his son, Roheem-Yar Khan, who had in the meantime returned from his mission to Sindh, to condole with them on their grievances. On their departure for Multan, on the retreat of the Sikhs, he presented them with clothes and money, amounting to one thousand rupees.

Soon afterwards, the Khan met with a very serious

accident, though fortunately not attended with any fatal result. It happened that as he was crossing the river Sutlej in a ferry-boat, on a hunting excursion, he was overtaken by a thunder-storm. The boat being unfit to withstand the tempest, went down with the Khan and his companions; but he, together with a few others, was saved by the ready aid of the boatmen, who carried them safely to the bank. The boatmen were richly rewarded, as they deserved, for their service.

A month afterwards, Sadik Khan received a letter from the honourable Mr. Elphinstone, on a perusal of which he expressed much joy, as it was sent by one of the most sincere well-wishers of his family.

About the same time, a letter was received from the governor of Bahawalpur, stating that the Sikhs were crossing to this side of the river, and were ravaging the surrounding territory. The matter was brought to the notice of Runjeet Sing, who took measures to prevent the incursions of the Sikhs.

About the middle of the year, the Khan received a visit from Gholam Hussain Khan, the nephew of Nawab Maeen-ud-Doula, of Dereh Ismael Khan. On his entry into Bahawalpur, he was received and conducted on his way by a deputation, consisting of the chief officers of the state. He was treated with honours suitable to his rank, although the visit was merely of a complimentary nature, as nothing else appears to have transpired on the occasion.

Shah Shuja, the ex-king, being about to proceed on an expedition against Cabul, again renewed overtures with Muzuffir Khan, to admit his family into Multan. In the beginning of August, the Nawab sent an agent to Sadik Khan, to take his advice on the matter; and as the latter advised him to accede to the Shah's wishes, the royal harem, admitted into Multan, was treated with due respect, and hospitably entertained during their stay.

The differences between the Kheirpur chief, and Sadik Mohammed, which had again been excited on account of the atrocities committed by the subjects of the two states against each other, were settled by the restoration of the cattle which had been reciprocally carried away.

About this period, a coldness appears to have taken place between the Khan, and Nasir Khan, his minister. The latter entertaining some fear regarding his own safety, opened a secret correspondence with Sohrab Khan, inviting him to attack and occupy the Bahawalpur territory, when he should be joined and assisted by Nasir Khan. This invitation was of course favourably received by the Kheirpur chief, and immediately communicated to his brethren of Hyderabad. The Meers, who had always been anxious to annex the Daoodputra territory to their own, readily availed themselves of the opportunity; and all the available troops were forthwith despatched in that direction. After effecting a junction with the Kheirpur forces, they attacked the Bahawalpur frontier, and began to plunder and to lay waste the surrounding country. The Subzul-Kot, as well as Khanpur and Ilahabad, were occupied without difficulty; and such was the rapidity with which the Sindhian chiefs prosecuted their measures, that Sadik Mohammed found himself quite unprepared to meet the exigency. To gain time, the Khan sent a deputation to temporise with the enemy; but being refused admittance into their camps, it returned without accomplishing its object. The Khan was therefore compelled to despatch as many troops as he could collect against the invaders, and to defend the remaining part of his territory, As soon as the two forces came in sight of each other, the Bahawalpur army was deserted, as had been previously arranged by Nasir Khan, of course to the great distress of his master. The Daoodputra troops, however, maintained their position, and had two or three short actions, but without gaining any advantage. In the meantime the enemy took possession of some more villages; and in this great emergency, the Khan was compelled to sue for peace, which was granted on condition of his elder son being sent to Hyderabad.*

On the 2nd of February, 1811, the young Khan proceeded with the Sindh army to Hyderabad, with presents to the chief of that place. He was treated with consideration; but was not allowed to leave the precincts of that town. Meanwhile, the Meers experienced a wish through an agent to the Khan, that he should give them the famous sword "Helal," which he had purchased from Sadik Ali Khan Kalabara, and which he esteemed as very valuable. The latter being very anxious for the return of his son, conquered his repug-

* Subzul-Kot remained in possession of the Sindhians, till it was restored by the British Government in 1843. On its occupation, Ismael Khan, the son of Subzul Khan, the founder, retired to Ahmedpur, where a few wells were assigned to him for his subsistence by the Khan, but taken back again on his death.

nance to part with this favorite sword, and sent it to them. On the receipt of it, the heir apparent was permitted to return to Bahawalpur, having been absent a year and a half at Hyderabad.

While the Khan was relieved from foreign invasion, his attention was engaged by the breaking out of a serious internal insurrection, which unexpectedly engaged him in hostilities with Multan. The events were as follows:—

Fatteh Mohammed Ghoree and Ahmed Khan, the two principal officers of his army, becoming, by some means, disaffected, conspired to assassinate their master, and to fill up his place by proclaiming one of his brothers as the chief of the state. A person named Sunjee Khan was selected by the conspirators to carry out the design. As the Khan was returning in the gloom of the evening from a ride at Ahmedpur, he was waylaid and attacked with a drawn sword by this savage marauder; but the camel on which he was mounted taking fright and accelerating its pace, he escaped and reached his residence in safety. Failing in this attempt, the assassin made his escape through the connivance of the attendants, who seem to have been in the conspiracy, and he was concealed in some secure place by the ringleaders. The Khan, apprehending further danger from the bad disposition of his officers and troops, proceeded the same night to the foot of Deirawer, giving orders to the malcontent troops to follow him thither. They obeyed the order; but on the day after their arrival, Fatteh Khan, Ahmed Khan, and Dhooman Sing, who had each under his command 500 horse and foot, quitted the place without notice, and proceeded towards Bahawalpur, to ravage that town. Osman Khan, however, the governor of the place, having become aware of their design, did not allow them to enter Bahawalpur; and being thus disappointed, they bent their course eastward, but being checked in that quarter also by some Daoodputra Jaghirdars, they were obliged to go across the river, and to wait on Surfaraz Khan, the elder son of Muzuffir Khan, who was the actual manager of his father's territory, and happened at that time to be at Shujabad. They succeeded in impressing on the weak mind of the young Nawab, that the power of the Khan had been much weakened by their desertion, and that his territory could be made an easy conquest, if he would only join them in attacking it. The young Khan, however, from politic motives, abstained from complying openly with their request, but he permitted them to ravage the Daoodputra Ilaka from his side of the river, in which they would be joined by the Afghans in his own service. When this circumstance was brought to the notice of the Khan, he remonstrated with Muzuffir Khan, in strong terms, for having given shelter to the rebels in his Ilaka. The Nawab, in reply, spoke of the Khan's own impropriety in allowing his troops to enter his territory. The Khan pleaded that he had despatched his troops merely to prevent the incursions of the rebels, but without any satisfactory result. In the meantime Yabe Mohammed Khan, an Afghan, who was likewise secretly discontented with his master, having been deputed by the Daoodputra court to Multan, to give a better explanation of the case, further excited the ambition of the Nawab, by convincing him of the general disaffection which he falsely represented as being prevalent among the Daoodputras against their chiefs, and by assuring him that the least hostile movement on his part, would make him the master of that country.

When another deputation arrived on the part of Bahawalpur, the Nawab charged the Khan with having ill-treated him by not answering, and by contemptuously throwing away many of his letters. He also dismissed the deputation without any decisive answer to the message of which it was the bearer, and at the same time deputed some emissaries to excite the Daoodputra feudatories, to rebel against their chiefs. For adopting this course, they were assured of the grant of additional Jaghirs, on the part of the Nawab. Some of them were led by these flattering promises to desert the territory and join the rebels; but the rest having loyalty still at heart, joined with the Khan's force in defending the territory. The Daoodputra army soon after advanced across the river, to punish the insurgents under the command of Mohammed Yakoob, who had been appointed Commander-in-chief. Such of the rebels as were plundering the surrounding country in scattered parties were driven back, and many of them were slain in the retreat.

The victorious force then advanced to attack Ahmed Khan, one of the chief rebels; who, on its approach, had shut himself up in the fort of Khanghru. After a feeble defence, however, feeling his inability to defend the place, he made his escape, when his followers surrendered at discretion and were allowed to retire without molestation.

Mortified at the ill-success of the rebels, Muzuffir Khan threw off the mask, and openly declared war against the Daoodputra chief. He first proceeded in person to Shujabad, and sent his army against Yakoob Mohammed Khan. The Multan force coming in contact with the advanced guard of his troops, easily put it to the rout; but the fugitives being joined by the main force, the action was renewed, and the Afghans were repulsed with great loss in killed and wounded; but having soon after received a reinforcement, they returned to the attack. The fight now became hotter, and much blood was shed on either side; but the advantage being on the side of the enemies, the Daoodputras were on the point of giving way, when they were providentially succoured by the arrival of a fresh detachment, under the command of Mohammed Daem Khan, and by a regular battalion, commanded by Captain Ashur Ali. They then maintained their ground, and a smart fire was opened, both from the guns and musquetry, which did severe execution in the ranks of the Afghans. The latter, however, not having the advantage of guns, left their horses loose, and made a general assault on the Daoodputras with drawn swords; but the fire from the Daoodputra artillery was so brisk and fatal, that they could not reach their opponents. Being thus weakened by the great loss which they suffered, they were attacked and overwhelmed by superior numbers, and were compelled to fly, leaving the Daoodputras masters of the field of battle. Many of the fugitives were hotly chased, and killed within a short distance. Ahmed Khan, the rebel, taking shelter behind an enclosure situated on a well, made a bold defence, but was at last put to the sword by the Daoodputras, together with fifty of his companions. His head was cut off and sent, for the satisfaction of Sadik Khan, to Deirawer. This last battle completed the defeat of the Multan army, and it retreated to Shujabad, to the great mortification of Muzuffir Khan; while the victors, overtaken by darkness, encamped on the field of battle. The next day, the dead of the enemy were transferred on hackeries to Shujabad, by the permission of the Daoodputra commander. Muzuffir Khan was of course extremely vexed at this severe reverse, and censured his advisers, although he himself was in fault for having originated this expedition.

While the two armies were thus engaged in hostile operations, Nawab Asud Khan, the new governor of Dereh Ghazi Khan, probably instigated by Muzuffir Khan, attacked the western frontier of the Daoodputra territory; and having established his garrison in Multan Kot and the fort of Schuwala, carried his ravages across the Indus, and laid waste a great many villages, carrying off, at the same time, the whole of the cattle belonging to the poor Ryots. On the return of the victorious army, the recovery of the above places, and the protection of the western frontier, were considered most essential; and Yakoob Khan, after being crowned with laurels for his glorious achievements, was soon afterwards despatched to that quarter, with a detachment of the victorious force and a few pieces of artillery. Asud Khan, however, feeling his inability to maintain his position, disgracefully retired to the seat of his government on the approach of the Khan's troops; withdrawing his garrisons at the same time from the occupied places. He moreover sent his son to Sadik Mohammed to apologise, and to ask pardon for his conduct, on payment of 50,000 rupees, for all the losses which had been suffered by the Daoodputra subjects, in consequence of his late incursion.

After reducing to peace this part of the territory, Yakoob Khan next proceeded to the southern frontier, which had also been disturbed and ravaged by Nasir Khan, the deserter. On his approach the latter retired, and tranquillity was now restored throughout the country. On his return to court, Yakoob Khan was distinguished by the grant of fresh laurels for his manly and judicious conduct.

Although superior force had put an end to the late hostile storm, yet the discontented spirit at home which had been at the bottom of it, was still further exasperated at the Khan's success. Khodayar Khan, who had been just pardoned for his late conspiracy, and Hajji Khan, his brother, were still secretly at work for his expulsion from the throne, and for raising Wahid Bukhsh, the elder son of the late Mobarik Khan, the rightful heir, to the Musnud. It afterwards appeared that they were also the chief movers of the late insurrection, and still kept up a correspondence with Fatteh Mohammed Ghoree, one of the rebel officers. The plot was matured; and the conspirators only waited for a favourable moment to carry it out. The absence of the Khan on the 24th of February, on a hunting excursion, furnished them with the desired opportunity; and their first step was to associate with themselves the officers commanding the garrison, by making them and their men large presents in money, and holding out favourable hopes for the future. The

Khan unfortunately not returning at night from the Shikaree, enabled the conspirators to prosecute their scheme at leisure. In the morning, Wahid Buksh was declared chief of the state, to the exclusion of Sadik Khan. The office of Vizir was assumed by Khodayar, and that of commander-in-chief was conferred on Hajji Khan. The gates of the fort were shut, the treasury seized, and a royal salute from the artillery announced the accession of the usurper. Gholam Hussain Khan, the Kidmutghar, and Salamut Rae the treasurer, who attempted to dissuade them from their design, were ordered to be killed. The former was accordingly put to the sword instantly, but the latter was saved through the intercession of some of the Harem.

The unusual report of the guns alarmed the Khan, who was engaged in hunting; and fearing something wrong, he immediately retraced his steps to the fort. On his approach, he was informed of the event by a Kidmutghar. Although much astonished at the occurrence, he yet maintained his presence of mind, and without loss of time held a consultation with his companions as to what was best to be done. They advised him to retire to Islamghur, in Cholistan, and there to collect an army for the punishment of the usurper. This plan was, however, disapproved of and rejected.

Had not Sadik found resources in his own abilities and address, he might have lost the state for ever. He decided that he could subdue his rebel brothers more easily while they were yet weak and wavering, than when still further strengthened in possession by consolidating the authority of their creatures. He also hoped that his presence might still work on the loyalty of his misled subjects and officers. Thus depending on his own discretion, the Khan at once proceeded to the fort. He was not disappointed in his hopes; for as soon as he made his appearance before the walls, the soldiers were ashamed to fire on their own master; and, to the great mortification of the rebels, suddenly left the fort, and joined Sadik, expressing their repentance. They were encouraged by a ready and general pardon, and invited to atone for their conduct, by making a brave attack on the fort. In the meantime, the troops having arrived from Ahmedpur, an assault was ordered, and the gates, which had already been seized by the return of the guards to their duty, were laid open: the troops entered without difficulty, and a general massacre ensued. The rebels were dispersed and put to the sword, with Khodayar and Hajji Khan. Wahid Buksh, to save his life, threw himself from the walls; but he was seized and slain by the Khan's people.

The Khan immediately held a public Durbar, and offered thanksgivings for his restoration to the throne. The event was announced by a royal salute in the fort, and by letters to distant officers. The troops, as they deserved, were at the same time handsomely rewarded for their loyal conduct.

Fatteh Mohammed Ghoree, who had all this time been anxiously waiting at Shujabad to hear of the progress of the above conspiracy, was entirely disappointed on hearing the result. He then proceeded to Multàn; but seeing no chance of any success there, he removed to Kheirpur, where Sohrab Khan took pity on him, and employed him in his service. In course of time he rose to the first rank in his court.

In the beginning of March, Sadik Mohammed moved towards Bahawalpur, and such of the Daoodputras as were still disaffected were deprived of their Jaghirs. They were, therefore, compelled to leave the country, and proceed to Hyderabad, where, through the medium of Nasir Khan, they succeeded in getting access to the Meers, and in moving them in their behalf, by the representations of their grievances. Nasir Khan proposed that if they would place a detachment of their forces at his disposal, he would undertake to have the exiled Daoodputras restored to their estates. The proposition was readily consented to; and the necessary arrangements were ordered to be made.

The matter, however, having come to the ears of the Khan, he apprehended a further disturbance of his territory, and was thereby convinced that as long as Nasir Khan remained at large, he could enjoy no peace; but, as gaining him over by forcible means was considered impracticable, he hit on a peaceable plan, and a deputation was therefore sent to the fugitive, to persuade him to come back, and to assure him that he was pardoned for his past conduct. Nasir Khan being, however, sensible of his misdemeanour, and besides, being well situated in the Kheirpur court, expressed his unwillingness to return. Successive agents were again sent to him to remove every suspicion from his mind; but as he yet hesitated, and all prolonged discussions had failed, a Khoran was forwarded by the Khan, with a sentence written on the leaf of the holy book, bearing his seal and signature, "that if Nasir Khan will return to the Bahawalpur Court, and will not act disloyally towards the state, he shall never be subjected to the displeasure of the Khan." On the presentation of this solemn engagement, Nasir Khan took leave of Sohrab Khan, and returned to Sadik Mohammed. He was apparently treated with the usual favour and consideration, and was reinstated in his old Jaghir of the village of Tarooda. For some time he was outwardly treated with marked kindness, but was, nevertheless, not restored to his rank at court. When at last he urged this point, he was treacherously summoned to Ahmedpur, and basely murdered by the Khan's order. His estate and property were, notwithstanding, bravely defended by his relatives and servants, about a hundred in number; but they were overwhelmed and butchered, both men and women, by the soldiery, while all the moveable property was removed to Ahmedpur, to satisfy the cupidity of the treacherous Khan.

To this horrid massacre a season of necessary inactivity succeeded, and the Khan appears to have enjoyed perfect peace for nearly two years and a half; for nothing worthy of record transpired during the interval, except the marriage of the heir apparent, Roheem Yar Khan, with the daughter of Kohneh Khan, a Daoodputra Jaghirdar. The nuptials were celebrated with due magnificence and pomp.

After the retreat of Vizir Fatteh Khan from Atok, in the middle of 1813, Mohammed Khan equipped another expedition, and proceeded in person at the head of his army to Dereh Ghazi Khan, to renew hostilities with the Sikhs. On his arrival in the latter place, he invited all the Mohammedan chiefs in that quarter to join in supporting him in this expedition. A deputation, consisting of Fatteh Khan his brother, Jubbar Khan, and Meer Mohammed Khan the chief of Khelat, was likewise sent to gain over Sadik to his cause. On the approach of the mission, the Khan, with the whole army in his pay as well as the Jaghirdars, proceeded to the left bank of the Indus, to meet it at the village Bhakree. He was, of course, on crossing the river received with due honour and respect. Besides this, on the Vizir's paying him a visit, the Khan vacated the Musnud, and made him sit on it, while he himself sat on the carpet with others. The mission remained three days, and was treated with every honour. The Khan not only readily agreed to obey his majesty's order in the projected expedition; but sent him a lakh of rupees as Nuzrana, besides a few choice horses and an elephant. The Vizir and the other members of the mission were presented with similar tokens of friendly regard on their departure. The Khan afterwards returned to Ahmedpur.

Towards the middle of 1814, Kazee Akil, the religious guide of the Khan, having died a natural death at Mithan-Kot, much lamentation ensued. The heir-apparent was also deputed on this occasion to console with his son and family on their loss. In the ensuing year, he proceeded in person to Mithan-Kot to observe the usual rites for the death of the late Kazee.

It is evident that great enmity had existed for a long while between the Kheirpur and Bahawalpur courts. The misunderstanding was now removed through the exertions of the well-wishers of both parties. Owing to the unfriendly terms on which they stood, Sohrab Khan had not yet performed the usual rites of condolence on the death of the late chief; but friendship having been now restored, he deputed his own grandson, Meer Mohammed Khan, with the usual presents for the Fateha-Khawanee, or reading the prayers for the dead. He was received and treated honourably; and on taking leave, was presented with valuable presents for himself and his grandfather. The brother of the Meer, Soleiman Khan, dying soon after, the compliment was returned by the Khan, by means of Azeem Khan, the second son of the Khan, who was sent on a deputation with the usual ceremonies.

Up to July, 1817, nothing is recorded beyond the death of a few of the Khans, when the usual ceremonies were performed.

The continued weakness and the decreased resources of Multan tempted Runjeet to renew hostilities against that place. In the beginning of 1818, the expedition was conducted by Dewan Nokhunchund, under the nominal control of Kharag Sing, the heir apparent. The citadel was for some time boldly defended, but at last was stormed and taken; Muzuffir Khan and his two sons were killed in the defence, and the place was sacked. A great quantity of booty fell into the hands of the victor; while Surfaraz Khan, his eldest son, who was vested with the management of the territory, and Zulfikar Khan, were conducted to Lahore, where Runjeet assigned them a small pension for their subsistence, and where they still continue. Ameer Boz Khan and Keihnamoz Khan, the grandsons of the late Nawab, took refuge at the same time at Bahawalpur under the protection of the Khan, where a suitable Jaghir was settled by the latter on them for their expenses.

Shah Shuja, who, on his escape from his confinement at Lahore, had taken shelter at Loodianah under the protection of the British Government in the commencement of 1819, arrived in the Bahawalpur territory on an expedition against Cabul. On his approach within nine koss of Ahmedpur, the Khan waited on his majesty and paid him every honour. He presented to him a Peishkush with 100 gold mohurs, besides 5,000 rupees with two well-caparisoned horses and one for riding, besides forty camels and an elephant. Numerous clothes, suitable presents, were at the same time presented to the princes, the sons of his majesty, and to his officers. The Khan in return was honoured by the grant of a horse and a shawl. Agreeably to the Shah's wishes, Sadik Mohammed placed at the disposal of his majesty a detachment of his own troops, under the command of Yakoob, to aid him in his present expedition. Thus assisted, the Shah crossed the river Sutlej, and advanced to attack Dereh Ghazi Khan. Samunder Khan, the Barukzaee governor, on his approach, marched out to oppose his majesty; and Zaman Khan, one of the chief officers, was ordered by the Shah to attack him. A smart engagement in consequence ensued, and the Shah's troops being overpowered, were about to give way, when Yakoob Khan, the commander of the Daoodputras, coming opportunely to their aid, turned the scales of victory in his majesty's favour. Samunder Khan was defeated and compelled to fly; and the Shah occupied the Dereh without further opposition. Yakoob Khan was distinguished by the grant of a Khelat, and moreover received thirty-nine wells in Jaghir, in consideration of his valuable service. Having thus effected the capture of the place, the Daoodputra troops returned to Ahmedpur; while the Shah, leaving the place in charge of Zaman Khan, himself proceeded to Peshawar. He was, however, not received cordially by the Afghans of that quarter, and was obliged to retrace his steps to the Dereh; but the governor refused allegiance, and did not allow him to enter the place. The Shah was, therefore, obliged to proceed thence to Shikarpur; but his presence not being liked by the Sindhians, he was compelled to return to Loodianah.

Towards the end of 1819, Runjeet Sing again appeared in person in the province of Multan, and thence carried on military operations across the Indus, and extended his authority as far as Bhakar, seizing a portion of the Khan's territory lying on the right bank of that river. Zaman Khan was at the same time expelled from Dereh Ghazi Khan, which was given in form, along with the newly conquered track of country, to Sadik Mohammed for three lakhs of rupees annually. Gholam Kader Khan was appointed by him to assume the charge of the territory; and in the beginning of the ensuing year, the Khan proceeded thither personally, and restored confidence to the people by his own presence for a few days.

Sullana, the famous freebooter, who, at the head of a troop of banditti of the Seal tribe, plundered and molested the surrounding country, was seized by the Khan's officers and confined in the fort of Islamghur in Cholistan.

After making the necessary arrangements and settling the country, the Khan returned to Ahmedpur, and thence to his residence at Deirawer.

Notwithstanding the seizure of Sullana, the Western frontier of Dereh Ghazi Khan still remained harassed and unsettled, by the restless incursions of the Beloochees occupying the skirt of the Western mountains. Troops were therefore sent in that direction to punish them on the opening of the next season. Their country was exposed to the ravages of the soldiery; and they were ultimately satisfactorily suppressed. Kora Khan, of the Khosa tribe, one of their principal leaders, was associated with the Khan, by giving him his daughter in marriage, and he was consequently reinstated in his Jaghir. The fort of Butree, one of their strongholds, was at the same time occupied; and three of its principal men were seized and carried prisoners to Ahmedpur, where they remained in confinement for some time.

About this time Gossaeen Beharjee, one of the chief functionaries of the Khan's state, died a natural death, being greatly regretted by the Khan. Jewan Ram, his son, was installed and confirmed in his place.

Owing to his declining health, the Khan does not seem to have been engaged for the rest of his life in any active or important action. His movements were confined within Ahmedpoor and Deirawer. Towards the end of 1825, his distemper began to increase, and no remedy could benefit him. His chief complaint was difficulty of respiration, which by degrees grew into confirmed asthma. He died at Deirawer, after a reign of sixteen years, on the 9th of Ramzan, 1241 (A.D. 1826), or in

April 1826, and was buried in the royal cemetery, much regretted by his family and dependants. On the same day he was succeeded by his elder son, Roheem Yar Khan, who has since then assumed the title of Bahawal Khan III.

The lease of the territory held on the right bank of the Sutlej and Indus, was renewed in his name with Runjeet Sing without much difficulty, and he continued to enjoy it till 1831, when it was resumed by Runjeet Singh, and governed by him directly.

THE BELOOCHEES.

It may be of some interest to know when the Beloochees left their old country, Cutch Mekran, and emigrated to their present position on the right bank of the Indus. It appears from the history, entitled "Heft Gulshun," that in the year 874 A.H. (A.D. 1459), when Behlal Lodee retired from his unsuccessful expedition against Multan, that Doodaee Hoot of the Beloochee tribe, who was Malek (king), left Mekran, with his sons, Ismael Khan and Fatteh Khan, and all his family, and arrived at Multan, and entered the service of Sultan Hussain, who then reigned as an independent chief in Multan. His territory in the West being incessantly harassed by the incursions of the neighbouring mountaineers, Sohrab Khan was considered a fit person to punish these freebooters. The tract of country lying between Kurwer and Dhein-Kot was, therefore, placed under his management. This intelligence induced many of his countrymen to emigrate from Mekran, and to join the Malek in his new settlement. The whole country lying on the right bank of the Indus, was afterwards assigned to the new settlers, in requital of their military services; and they have enjoyed ever since the possession of that tract of country. The story given by the oldest inhabitants of Multan and Dereh Ghazi Khan, of the settlement of the Beloochees in this country, is as follows.

On the arrival of Sohrab Khan in Multan, he was joined by Hajji Khan and Ghazi Khan, together with many other Beloochees. When the lands on the Western bank of the Indus were assigned, in lieu of their pay, to Sohrab and Hajji Khan, the former founded the town of Ismael Khan, and the latter, that of Dereh Ghazi Khan. In the reign of Sultan Mohammed, the grandson of Sultan Hussain, when the Multan government began to decline, Ghazi Khan took possession of the whole Khalsa lands, and made himself an independent chief. On his death he was succeeded by his son Hajji Khan, who extended his territory still further, and placed his power on a firmer basis. It was customary among the Dereh chiefs to adopt alternately the title of Ghazi Khan and Hajji Khan. This dynasty continued without interruption in the territory for ten successive generations, and was also confirmed by the Mogul emperors. In the year 1152, A.H. (A.D. 1737), on the invasion of Nadir Shah, Dereh Ghazi Khan was separated from the Mogul territory, with other places to the north-west of the Indus, and was annexed to the Persian empire. The present dynasty was, however, confirmed by Nadir Shah also. In the year 1172 (A.D. 1757), Ghazi Khan X. dying without issue, the Dereh was then made an integral part of the Cabul empire, which had been just formed on the dismemberment of the kingdom established by Nadir, and was governed directly. Koramul was the first governor who was appointed by Ahmed Shah Durranee, and he was succeeded by Gholam Shah Khaloora, the ruler of Hyderabad, who governed the district for sixteen years. He was followed by Zaman Khan in the time of Timur Shah, who continued to govern for three years, when he was succeeded by Mirza Khan Alukzaee, who governed the district for nine years, and was superseded by Samunder Khan Barukzaee. Sunder Khan, the son of Mirza Khan, followed him, but had the charge only for a short time. On the accession of Shah Zaman, Asud Khan, the brother of Vizir Fatteh, was nominated to the government of the Dereh, and after two years was succeeded by Ahmed Khan Populzaee. After this, the districts, owing to the fluctuating state of the Cabul empire, had alternately several governors, viz., Sheikh Gum-ud-Deen, Ibrahim Khan, Populzaee, Samunder Khan, and Jubbar Khan, the step-brothers of Fatteh Khan, Habibullah Khan Suddoozye, Mohammed Zaman Khan Barukzaee, and Samunder Khan, during the reigns of Shah Zaman, Shah Shuja, and Shah Mohammed. In the year 1230 (A.D. 1815), the district was captured by Runjeet, and leased to the Bahawalpur chief. In 1247 (A.D. 1832), it was taken back and placed in charge of General Ventura, one of the French officers in the Maharajah's service. He managed it for two years; and it was afterwards annexed to Multan and governed by Sowanmul-Nore Mulraj, whose son is now governor.

Ibrahim Khan and Mohammed Yar Khan, two of the relations of Ghazi Khan, are yet alive, and living at Dereh Ghazi Khan. The income of only two wells is assigned to them for their subsistence. The Beloochees have no history of their own extant, and hence the imperfect condition of this account may claim excuse.

SUPPLEMENTARY ACCOUNT OF THE DAOODPUTRAS.

[The following account of the Daoodputras is from a different authority to that of the preceding pages, and though it repeats much of a similar character, yet as it serves to confirm or correct what has been stated, it has been thought useful to insert it.]

THE Daoodputras, especially that branch of the tribe of which Bahawal Khan is the head, claim descent from Huzrut Abbas, the uncle of the prophet Mohammed (the Khan is styled Mohammed Bahawul Khan, Abbassee) Their real origin is to be traced to a very different source. Their progenitor, Daood, was a resident of Shikarpur of the class called Julahas, or weavers. He is said to have had five sons, Arab, Abbas, Hussun, Hasib and Casim; from the four first are descended the Arbanee, Abbassee, Husseinee, and Hisbanee Daoodputras. Daood and his sons were much skilled in the use of the rifle, and spent more of their time in pursuit of game than they devoted to working at the loom. Being successful sportsmen, the sale of their game enabled them to live much beyond the means of their neighbours; and an occasional distribution of it in presents to their friends, gained them a name and ascendancy, which eventually became formidable to the ruling authorities.

Abbas, one of the sons of Daood, had a son called Pirij. The wife of this man absconded with one Kahur (a Hullal-khor), by whom she had several male children. The friends of the husband, after a lapse of some years, on discovering her hiding-place, took the life of Kahur, and restored the woman with her sons to her husband's family. From the sons borne by this woman to her paramour, Kahur, are descended the Kehranee branch of the Daoodputras; and from the sons she bore to her husband Pirij (son of Abbas), the Abbassee or *Pirjanee* branch.

The tribe branches out into various other subdivisions or families; but the chief are, as mentioned above, and in the following order:—The Arbanee, Abbassee or Pirjanee, Hussunee, Hisbanee, and Kehranee. As they became numerous, they gradually relinquished their more industrious occupation of weavers, and devoted themselves more exclusively to the use of arms. Many took service under the Nazims of Multan and Tatta, and under the emperors of Delhi; but the greater number remained to infest the roads between Shikarpur and Multan, plundering Kafilas, and committing depredations on every side.

It is not, however, until the time of the Emperor Aurungzeb, that we have any authentic mention of them. When Shazada Moiz-ud-Deen, the emperor's son, who was Nazim of Multan, engaged in an expedition to punish a revolt of the Belooch tribes on the right bank of the Indus, a tribe, called the Daoodputras, are said to have come to him to complain of the oppression of Noor Mohammed Khan, governor of Tatta (Hyderabad and Shikarpur), against whose authority they had rebelled, and from whom they had just suffered a severe chastisement. Mobarik Khan was then the acknowledged leader of this tribe. It happened that during their stay in prince Moiz-ud-Deen's camp, the Beloochees made a night-attack on the prince's Harem-sera, with a view to plunder it. The guards deserted their posts, and the Beloochees would have effected their purpose but for the opportune interference of a party of Daoodputras, who, led on by their chief Mobarik Khan, succeeded in putting the Beloochees to flight. For this signal service (for the prince acknowedged that he owed the preservation of his honour to their courage), they obtained a Jaghir in the vicinity of Shikarpur.

The next mention of them occurs about forty years later on the return of Nadir Shah from Hindustan, when a party of Daoodputras conducted his forces to Oomerkote in pursuit of Khodree Yar Khan (*i. e.* Noor Mohammed Khan), governor of Sindh. On this occasion, in A.D.1744, Sadik Mohammed Khan, son of Mobarik Khan, accompanied Nadir Shah on his return to Persia, from whence he was dismissed with great honours and with the grant of additional lands for himself and his tribe in the vicinity of Shikarpur.

Although Sadik Mohammed Khan appears to have been the ostensible chief of the whole tribe, there were others sharing little less consideration than himself in the different branches or families to which they belonged; among these the most considerable were Maroof Khan, Ummur Khan, and Noroz Khan, afterwards known as the Kheirpur Daoodputras.

In consequence of Sadik Mohammed Khan appropriating to himself and family a larger share of the lands bestowed by Nadir Shah than was warranted by the rules which had hitherto guided the conduct of the different branches of the tribe towards each other, these chiefs determined to separate themselves from their brethren, and seek their fortunes elsewhere. With this intention they crossed over to the left bank of the Indus, accompanied by their families and in fact the greater number of the tribe. Meeting no opposition, they proceeded peaceably up the left bank of the Punjnud and Sutlej, till they arrived at Kheirpur, where, with the permission of the authorities, they formed a settlement, hiring land from the Naib of Hasilpur (then the seat of authority), and engaging in cultivation.

Soon after this event, which occurred in the beginning of A. D. 1745, a desperate feud arose between Sadik Mohammed Khan, the chief of that branch of the tribe which had remained at Shikarpur, and the governor of the place, owing to the latter having forcibly possessed himself of the affianced bride of Sadik Mohammed Khan's eldest son, Bahawal Khan. Sadik Mohammed Khan finding himself too weak, after the division of his own tribe, to oppose the governor, sent his son Bahawal Khan to his brethren at Kheirpur, to state the insult which had been offered to all the tribe in his person, and to beg of them to return and revenge him. Bahawal Khan remained for two years a petitioner at their doors, without obtaining his object. At length they relented, forgot the injuries they had suffered from his father, and returned with him to Shikarpur, where they immediately raised a rebellion against Bakhtyar Khan, the governor, overthrew him, and restored the bride to her family. But not contented with satisfying their revenge, they plundered the city of Shikarpur, drove out the inhabitants, and commenced laying the country far and near under contributions. When intelligence of these disturbances reached Nadir Shah, he sent a large force under one of his generals (called in native accounts Tamasp Coolee), to reduce the Daoodputras to obedience. The Daoodputras, on the news of his arrival, fled with their families, and crossed over to the left bank of the Indus, where they were pursued by Tamasp. Impeded in their flight by their families, and seeing but little hope of escape, they determined on trying the chance of a battle, and, as is usual with them on these occasions, they sacrificed the greater number of their women and children before the engagement. A few were allowed to live, and proved of the greatest assistance in bringing water to their harassed husbands during the battle, which is said to have lasted the whole day. The distress of the opposite party for want of water contributed to their defeat. The Daoodputras completely routed them, and plundered the camp of the Persian leader.

After this exploit, they did not dare to return to Shikarpur; but, continuing their course along the left bank of the Indus, most of them settled at Allahabad. The branch of the tribe which had left Kheirpur to assist their friends, returned to the vicinity of that place. Bahawal Khan, with the Pirjanee branch of the tribe, soon left the country near Allahabad, and advanced higher up till he came to the spot on which the city of Bahawalpur now stands; and there laid the foundation of the city which is called after his name. In the short space of two years, the whole country between the desert and the river, and extending along the banks from Subzul-Kot, on the Indus, to near Mobarikpur, on the Sutlej, acknowledged and submitted to their rule. The country round Bahawalpur, which fell more immediately to the share of Bahawal Khan, extended in length about one hundred koss, varying in breadth from five to fifteen.

This chief might, with propriety, be called the Founder of the family, as he was the founder of their power on this side the river; they prefer, however, tracing their title to the name of rulers, or Sahib-i-Mulk, to his father, Sadik Mohammed Khan, the first who received a royal grant of land from Nadir Shah.

Bahawal Khan I. is said to have been a benevolent man, simple in his manners, and mild in his rule. He encouraged persons of all descriptions to settle at Bahawalpur, which, from being a Jhonk, or feeding-place for cattle, dotted with a few hamlets, soon increased to a flourishing town. He extended the frontier of his territory in the desert to beyond the fort of Dilawer, which he took from a relative of the Bikaner Raja. The descendants of its former possessor still reside at Bikaner.

To the north-east frontier, the Daoodputras of Kheirpur, Koth Caim Raees, and Hasilpur, possessed themselves at the same time of the forts of Rakkenpur, Majghur, Marroth, Tihara, and Pholehra, from the Bikaner Raja; while those of Gurhee and Hurrur made themselves masters of the forts of Deenghur and Islamghur belonging to the Raja of Jeyselmeer. These forts afterwards served them as strongholds, and places of refuge, whenever they were threatened by forces from without.

Bahawal Khan continued to rule about ten years. He had two brothers, Mobarik Khan, and Fatteh Khan, and dying without issue, was succeeded by the elder, Mobarik Khan, a chief of great ability and enterprize.

Mobarik Khan, after strengthening his frontier to the north-east, by erecting a strong fort at Mobarikpur, subdued the country along the left bank of the river as far as the Muzuffiran Wala; and, on the opposite side from ten miles west of Pakpatan and Kot Kubboala, to the fort of Tibbee, Lukkoke, and Summe Saldire. During his rule, the Daoodputras of Hasilpur, Koth, and Kheirpur, took possession of the country on the opposite side of the river dependent on Multan, up to Duneapur and Kheirur. From those places to the banks of the Chenab, Mobarik Khan rented from Shuja Khan and Muzuffir Khan, the Nawabs of Multan; while the country dependent on the Dereh, from Kunjer to Lalpur, between the Indus and the Chenab, Ghazi Khan rented from the Subahdar of that place under the Cabul sovereigns. At the same time that he acquired this great accession of territory on the right bank of the Sutlej, he humbled the pride, and circumscribed the power of the chiefs of the rival branches of his tribe within his own dominions. He died without issue, after having ruled for fifteen years; but, previous to his death, he appointed Jaffer Khan, the son of his brother, Fatteh Khan, for his successor, bestowing on him at the same time the name of Bahawal Khan.

Bahawal Khan, the second of the name, is represented to have been a wise and good ruler. He gave great encouragement to trade; and during his time, Bahawalpur vied with Multan in the manufacture of silk cloths, Shatrinjees, woollen rugs and carpets. To the east of the Muzuffiran Wala, he added to his territory the districts of Gunjiana and Rana Watto, which he took from Bhaee Lal Sing, the Keital Wala Sirdar. The fort of Walhur, in the desert, belonging to the Bikaner Raja, also fell into his hands. His revenues are said to have amounted to upwards of thirty-four lakhs of rupees, and his power had increased in proportion. He discontinued the tribute which had been hitherto paid to the Nazims of Multan, and Ghazi Khan of Dereh, for the territory rented from them, and exacted tribute from the heads of all the other branches of his tribe for the country which they held. His growing power had long excited the jealousy of his brethren, the Kheirpur Daoodputras, who joined with the Nazims of Multan, and Ghazi Khan of Dereh, in sending frequent complaints of his encroachments to the court of Timur Shah, and begged that a force might be sent to curb him. In the year 1784, A.D., after the revolt of the Talpuras in Sindh, which Sirdar Muddud Khan was sent to quell, the same general received orders to settle the affairs of the Derahjat and Multan. His operations, however, against the Daoodputras appear to have ended in idle threats and admonitions, which were little attended to by the Bahawalpur chief; and the army sent under Ahmed Khan Noorzai two years afterwards, after being defeated by the Talpuras, was unable to shew face to the Daoodputras. At length Timur Shah himself, in 1788, marched with a large army to awe the Daoodputra chief into subjection. Bahawal Khan, on the news of the Shah having crossed the Indus, fled to the desert with his family and treasures; these he placed in the fort of Khanghur, twenty koss east from Dilawer, and himself and his army continued wandering about, daily changing their ground, in order the better to elude pursuit.

Timur Shah, after plundering and laying waste the city of Bahawalpur, proceeded directly on to Dilawer to capture that fort. In this measure, he was guided by the advice of the Daoodputras, who had joined his army to oppose the Khan. As Dilawer was supposed to be the place in which Bahawal Khan kept his treasures, the Shah was the more anxious for its capture, and spared no trouble to effect it. The garrison made an obstinate resistance; and the Shah's artillery, after three days' battering, made little impression on its solid mud walls. Great distress was experienced in the Shah's army from the scarcity of water; the fort was, however, ultimately taken, but after a great sacrifice of life. Nothing could exceed the Shah's disappointment in not finding any of the treasure which he expected; and his wrath against the Daoodputras, who had advised him to besiege the fort, knew no bounds.

Timur Shah, thinking it madness to pursue the Khan any farther into the desert, and unable to subsist his army where he was, had no alternative but to retire upon Bahawalpur. Here he tried every means of negotiation, by promises and threats, to induce Bahawal Khan to consent to a meeting, but without effect. Muzuffir Khan, Nawab of Multan, and Mukdoom Gunj Buksh, a celebrated Peer of Uch, were the messengers employed on this occasion. The Khan resisted all overtures, till he himself became distressed for the means of supporting his followers in the desert. He then reluctantly consented to send his eldest son, Wahid Buksh, as a hostage for his own future peaceable conduct. Accordingly, Wahid Buksh, after receiving the propitious name of Mobarik Khan, forthwith proceeded to join the Shah. On his arrival, Timur Shah set out on his return to Cabul, where weightier affairs demanded his presence, happy at retiring so well out of a business in which he latterly contemplated nothing but disaster and disgrace. He left the entire settlement of the Khan's country to Muzuffir Khan, Nawab of Multan; and with the exception of a small body of troops under Sirdar Khan, an Afghan, which was left to garrison Dilawer, crossed the Indus with the whole of his army. He had not, however, passed Dereh Ghazi Khan, when intelligence reached him that Bahawal Khan had returned from the desert, surprised and put to death the garrison left at Dilawer; and passing through Ahmedpur, had arrived on the banks of the Indus, the people submitting to him as he advanced.

However exasperated the Shah may have been at this conduct, he does not appear to have resented it further than by investing Mobarik Khan, the son of Bahawal Khan, with full powers over the country ruled by his father. This he did on dismissing him, when he conferred upon him the title of Sirbaland Khan, and loaded him with handsome presents, taking from him at the same time a written engagement for the due payment of tribute for that part of the territory which was rented from the Nazims of Multan, and Dereh Ghazi Khan.

The Daoodputras, who had joined the Shah against Bahawal Khan, and conducted his army to Dilawer, were, on the contrary, treated with the utmost rigour. The Shah never forgave them for taking him on that bootless adventure; and ascribed the Khan's obstinacy in not surrendering himself, to the accounts which they forwarded to him of the distress of the Shah's troops. On leaving

Dereh Ghazi Khan, the Shah committed them to the care of the Nawab of that place (Shah Mohammed Khan Buddozaee) with orders to keep them in close confinement.

Whether Bahawal Khan was incensed at his son, Mobarik Khan, on account of the honours conferred on him to his own prejudice, or whether he had good reasons to suspect his designs is uncertain; but no sooner did he return, than he was put into close confinement, which continued during the life-time of his father. Immediately on his son's return, Bahawal Khan crossed the river; and before Timur Shah had reached Peshawar, he had defeated the Nawab of Multan, laid siege to Dereh Ghazi Khan, and released his brethren, the Daoodputras, from imprisonment. In this expedition he was assisted by the Peer of Uch, Mukdoom Gunj Buksh, a man of singular energy, and possessed of great influence in the country. He brought back with him to Bahawalpur several of the guns which had been taken from him by Timur Shah, and left with Muzuffir Khan, and others which he captured from Shah Mohammed Khan.

This campaign was followed by three years of uninterrupted tranquillity, during which the Khan occupied himself in the internal improvement of his country, and in strengthening himself against his enemies. Canals were cut from the river through such parts of the country as were sterile, and thinly inhabited, in order to induce people to settle on them. The builder of a well was allowed to enjoy rent-free as much land as it would enable him to cultivate for the period of four years. Merchants and artificers of every description were invited to settle at the different towns; and a considerable trade is said to have existed at Kheirpur, Bahawalpur, and Cawnpur, on the south-western frontier. A gun-foundry was established at Bahawalpur, and work in iron at that place carried to a perfection which was unknown either at Lahore or Multan. The rifle barrels made there surpass anything of the kind made elsewhere in India.

The disturbed state of the Punjaub, and of the country on the right bank of the Indus during this period, drove numbers of the more peaceful inhabitants to seek an asylum elsewhere; and the mildness of the Khan's government, for which he was deservedly famed, attracted great numbers to settle in his country. Similar causes conduced to bring the greater part of the trade of Afghanistan with Central India into this channel; and Bahawalpur became a great place of resort to the Lohanee merchants, where they exchanged their goods for the produce of India.

This period, when internal tranquillity had produced security from without, may be considered the most prosperous of the Daoodputra rule; it was not, however, destined to continue. The chiefs of Gurhee Ikhtyar Khan on the one side, and those of Kheirpur, Koth, and Hasilpur on the other, watched with unceasing jealousy the strength which Bahawal Khan was acquiring from the tranquil and flourishing state of his dominions. They not unjustly conceived that his power would soon overwhelm that of all the smaller chiefs, unless some effectual check was opposed to him. Their former bad success did not prevent their renewing their plots against him, and making fresh inroads into his territory. Armed bodies were sent to seize the cattle and property of his subjects; and the Zemindars incited to refuse the payment of their rents. These attempts were at first checked by threats and remonstrances on the part of the Khan, and by restitution being exacted from the offenders: but they gradually assumed a more formidable aspect; and the rival chiefs received an accession to their strength in the revolt of the Peer of Uch, Mukdoom Gunj Buksh, which induced them to set the Khan at open defiance. There can be no doubt that the Khan had given just cause of complaint to his brethren, and more especially to the Peer, and that nothing but his fears had hitherto restrained him from depriving them of their land; but it may be doubted, whether, by the measures they pursued, they were not precipitating the fate which they had to dread, when an opposite conduct would have averted it for an indefinite period. Mukdoom Gunj Buksh raised an army against the Khan, and at one time got possession of the person of Mobarik Khan, whom he released from confinement, and set up in opposition to his father. An engagement took place between them, in which the Khan's forces were defeated; and had there been any union of interest among his enemies, the struggle would have terminated fatally to his power; but this was not the case, and a knowledge of their obstinate feuds and jealousies enabled the Khan, even when almost without an army, to turn the scales in his favour. He then became the aggressor; one chief after another was subdued, their forts were destroyed, and they themselves, despoiled of their lands, were obliged to flee for safety into the territory of the neighbouring states. It was the boast of Bahawal

Khan that he left not a man among his brethren in his territory who would be able hereafter to disturb the welfare of his government, or dispute his absolute authority. Those who had submitted to him and remained, were content to sink into obscurity, and receive a charitable pittance for their subsistence. The power of these families has never revived; a few of their descendants are still pensioners on the bounty of the present Khan, while others are dispersed among the people, and their origin forgotten.

Bahawal Khan II. died in the year 1811, after having sat on the Musnud upwards of forty years. It was during this chief's time in 1808-9, that the Hon. M. Elphinstone passed through Bahawalpur on his mission to Cabul. When the Khan was reproached by his minister for the lavish expenditure of his entertainment to a passing stranger who was not likely ever to be of any use to him, he is said to have rebuked him for his want of foresight, telling him, "that though he might not derive advantage from it, his successors would; for it was written in the Koran, that the power of the Feringees should extend over the whole of India."

Bahawal Khan left seven sons to dispute the succession; viz.: Mobarik Khan (before mentioned), Abd-ullah Khan, Khoda Yar Khan, Nasir Khan, Hajji Khan, Kader Buksh Khan, and Firoz Mohammed Khan. Immediately after his death, his ministers, Nasir Khan Beloochee Goorgez, Missur Khan Beloochee Goorgez, and Fatteh Mohammed Khan Ghoree, who had been chiefly instrumental in effecting the confinement of the eldest son, Mobarik Khan, and were naturally alarmed at the prospect of his succeeding to power, entered into a conspiracy to set him aside in favour of the second son, Abd-ullah Khan, to whom they gave the preference over all the rest, as being the least ambitious and the weakest; and therefore the one most likely to submit to their guidance. In order the better to accomplish their object, they placed him on the musnud before the funeral obsequies were performed for his father, and spread a report at the same time of the death of Mobarik Khan, whom they sent people to murder. They obliged the remaining five brothers to acknowledge the authority of Abd-ullah Khan, and immediately afterwards placed them again in confinement.

Abd-ullah Khan, on succeeding to the Musnud, was surnamed Sadik Mohammed Khan (the second of the name). He was a weak man, the creature of his ministers, and exercised a very feeble authority in his country. The chief traits of his character were a penurious disposition and great avarice.

The Ameers of Sindh, who had long asserted a claim to the Khote of Subzul Khan, but had hitherto been restrained from enforcing it, by their respect for the power of Bahawal Khan, thought the weakness of the present ruler a favourable opportunity for doing so. They accordingly assembled an army and marched towards the frontier. Sadik Mohammed Khan was not slow in making preparations to resist them, and he advanced to encounter them with a superior force. They came to an engagement, and the Khan's troops fled from the first onset of their enemies. They were supposed to be disaffected, owing to their being badly paid and much in arrears. The Khan's ministers, however, succeeded in rallying them on the next day; and, by the promise of handsome rewards and better pay, persuaded them to encounter the Sindhians a second time. In this action, the army of the Ameers was totally defeated; the Wuzeers pursued their advantage till they drove them beyond the frontier, and returned with their victorious troops to the Khan's camp. Instead, however, of meeting with the reward which they merited, the Khan, now thinking himself rid of his enemies, treated his troops with the same neglect as heretofore—a conduct which exasperated them to open rebellion.

The commanders of the Ameer's forces, informed of this disaffection through their spies in the Khan's camp, and anxious to wipe out the memory of their recent defeat, lost no time in reassembling their army, and again entering the Khan's territory. Sadik Khan once more prepared to oppose them; but his troops deserted him and dispersed, refusing to encounter the Sindhians, and he saved himself by flight. The Sindhians ravaged the whole country, from Subzul Khote to Ahmedpur and Uch on the left bank of the river, and to Sutpur on the opposite bank. Here their progress was for some days arrested by a force hastily assembled from Kheirpur, under Chunnee Khan Daoodputra, which allowed the Khan time to offer terms to the commanders of the Sindhian army.

They agreed to withdraw from his territory on his paying them one lakh of rupees, resigning all claim to the fort of Subzul Khan, and sending his eldest son, Roheem Yar Khan, as a guarantee of his sincerity, to the Ameers. The Khan consented to their proposal, and Roheem Yar

Khan, the present Bahawal Khan, accompanied the Sindhee force to Hyderabad, where he was well received by the Ameers; and, after a short time, dismissed with handsome presents, to return to his father.

The weakness of Sadik Khan's government, lost him much of the territory which his predecessors had gained with the sword, while his inattention to affairs caused considerable diminution in the revenue of the territory which he retained. Trade declined under the extortions practised by his officers, which he was too indolent to check. He was much governed by the advice of his ministers, Nasir Khan Goorgez and Fatteh Mohammed Ghoree; and perhaps the best act of his life was his attempt to rid himself of their authority. They were obliged to save themselves by flight. Nasir Khan was afterwards induced to return on the promise of the Khan to restore him to favour; but he no sooner put himself into the Khan's power, than his life paid the forfeit of his temerity. His family and dependants were all massacred, and his house was plundered of the property he was supposed to have amassed in the Khan's service.

Fatteh Mohammed Ghoree was aided in his escape by the troops sent to apprehend him, who thus shewed their gratitude for his liberality, of which they had often partaken. He carried with him his family, and fled to Multan; from there he went to Lahore, to the court of Runjeet Sing; but getting no employment, two years afterwards proceeded to Sindh, to Meer Sohrab, chief of Kheirpur, who invested him with the office of minister, which he continues to hold to this day, under the present chief, Meer Rustum.

The place of these ministers was supplied by Sheik Deen Mohammed and his sons, Sheik Mukbool and Sheik Noor Mohammed, who appear to have enjoyed the Khan's confidence without abusing it as their predecessors had done. Nothing but their excellent management enabled the Khan at all to regulate the demands of the Lahore chief for tribute, which were daily becoming more urgent and excessive.

Sadik Khan's father, Bahawal Khan, after he had discontinued paying tribute to Muzuffir Khan, Nawab of Multan, and to the Nazim of Dereh Ghazi Khan, entered into a treaty with the Lahore chief, by which he bound himself not to assist Muzuffir Khan, and the Lahore chief bound himself not to demand tribute from Bahawal Khan if ever Multan fell into his possession. Runjeet Sing proceeded three times against Multan during the life of Bahawal Khan, always levying a Peishkush or tribute, but never permanently occupying the country. In 1818, he established his authority throughout the territory, and in 1821, subdued the country round the Dereh; and, soon after Bahawal Khan's death, he demanded tribute from Sadik Mohammed Khan. The Khan refused it, and assembled an army on the right bank of the Sutlej, to resist the threatened invasion of his territory. An action took place near the fort of Tibbee, in which the Khan's troops were defeated; and the Maharajah then exacted a tribute of 700,000 rupees, and demanded a Nuzrana of one lakh of rupees yearly, as the price of his forbearing to make aggression on the Khan's dominions. The Nuzrana was finally settled at 50,000 rupees; but, on subduing the country round Dereh Ghazi Khan, the Maharajah raised his demand to a lakh, then to a lakh and a half, and two lakhs: it was, however, only nominally so, and never levied without a military demonstration on the part of the Lahore chief; which, as often as it occurred, was the signal for the Khan's officers in authority on the opposite side of the river to abandon the country, and cross over to this side, leaving as little property as possible to be pillaged by their marauding invaders. A compromise generally occurred for less than half the sum demanded, when the Sikhs retired, leaving the country each time less capable than before of satisfying their increased demands on it. This state of affairs continued until after the death of Sadik Mohammed Khan.

The Bahawalpur chiefs have never paid tribute to any power for their possessions on the left bank of the Sutlej and Indus. Mobarik Khan paid a rent-charge of 70,000 rupees to the Cabul sovereign through the Nazim of Dereh Ghazi Khan for the country which he farmed from him in that neighbourhood, and 70,000 rupees for that farmed from the Nawab of Multan. Bahawal Khan II. discontinued the payment of this tribute. Timur Shah conferred the government of the Bahawalpur state on Mobarik Khan during the lifetime of his father Bahawal Khan, and on that occasion made him acknowledge himself a subject and tributary of the Cabul sovereignty. But these terms were dictated to him probably as the price of his release; and, so far from being assented to by Bahawal Khan, formed the chief grounds of his displeasure against his son, and his plea for putting him into confinement. Sadik Mohammed Khan transferred the payment of the tribute from the

Nawab of Multan, and of the Nazim of Dereh Ghazi Khan, to Runjeet Sing, when he became possessed of these countries.

Sadik Mohammed Khan had many enemies; and once, during his absence on a hunting excursion from Dilawer, a circumstance occurred which was near depriving him of his power. Some men of influence in the tribe joined his five brothers in a conspiracy to depose him; the brothers escaped from their imprisonment, overpowered and murdered their guards, and made themselves masters of the fort of Dilawer. The Khan was not five miles from Dilawer when this happened. News was immediately conveyed to him, before the mischief had time to spread; but his timidity got the better of every other feeling, and he prepared for flight. He was, however, persuaded by his adherents to wait till evening; in the meantime to send a party to Dilawer to ascertain the feeling of the people. Mohammed Daim Khas Kheilee was trusted with the direction of this party. He proceeded to Dilawer with a number of the Khan's Rohilla guard and other troops, and summoned the conspirators in the fort to surrender. A battalion of the Khan's regular infantry, chiefly Sipahis from the eastward, who had not been invited to join the conspirators, and were posted outside the fort, immediately came over to him; and he then sent off a message to the Khan to ask permission to attack the fort. The Khan, on receiving this message, went in person with the rest of his followers to Dilawer. His Rohilla guard, about four hundred men, led the way in an attack on the fort, and rushed with such violence against the gates as to carry them from their hinges.

An entrance once gained, the numbers on the Khan's side prevailed, and he found himself once more in possession of power. Such, however, was the fright he had received, that he is said to have remained inside his harem for a month afterwards, afraid to allow any one to approach him from without. He gave orders that three of his brothers, Khodayar Khan, Hajji Khan and Firoz Mohammed Khan, and two sons of his brother Mobarik Khan, should be put to death. Nasir Khan and Kader Buksh Khan, his two remaining brothers, were spared, from the strong evidence of their being unwilling accomplices in the treason.

Sadik Mohammed Khan died in the year in 1825, and was succeeded by his eldest son, Roheem Yar Khan, surnamed Mohammed Bahawal Khan, the present ruler.

Almost the first act of this chief on succeeding to the Musnud was to rid himself of his father's ministers, Sheik Mukbool and Sheikh Noor Mohammed. This was done at the instigation of the Khas Kheilee Mohammed Yakoob, Mohammed Kaim and Mohammed Daim, the same persons who had instigated Sadik Mohammed Khan to take the life of his ministers Nasir Khan Goorgez and Fatteh Mohammed Ghoree, and to possess himself of their property. Mohammed Yakoob at this time held the appointment of Meer Bukshee, or paymaster to the forces; and his uncles, Mohammed Kaim and Mohammed Daim, inferior offices in the Khan's household; but from the circumstance of their being Gholams, whose fortunes had risen with the fortune of the Khan's family, they were always considered as highly trustworthy, and were employed in affairs of secresy and importance. They appear, however, to have used their influence towards their own aggrandisement with little regard for the true interests of their master.

They persuaded the Khan that his ministers, Sheik Mukbool and Sheikh Noor Mohammed, were hatching a conspiracy to depose him in favour of his younger brother Azeem Yar Khan. The Khan was the more willing to give credence to this story, from his having had many misunderstandings with them during the lifetime of his father, when there might have been grounds for suspecting them of not being favourable to his cause. It was generally known that the younger brother, Azim Yar Khan, was a greater favourite with the people, and a man in every respect better qualified to rule than Bahawal Khan, who was never remarkable for his abilities, and had shewn much of the distrustful and parsimonious disposition of his father. But, however ill-disposed the ministers might have been to Bahawal Khan during his father's life, they appear to have become reconciled to his succession; otherwise the death of Sadik Mohammed Khan would have been their time for espousing the cause of the younger son, Azeem Yar Khan. Instead of doing this, they proclaimed Bahawal Khan the successor to his father, and immediately after placed Azeem Yar Khan in confinement. But whether culpable or not in their intentions towards the Khan, the motives of their accusers are sufficiently obvious. These men, the Khas Kheilee, as they are termed, possessed a great influence over the Khan's mind, and saw in the ministers the only obstacle to their attainment of a power commensurate with that influence; they, therefore, raised the Khan's avarice by accounts of the wealth which the ministers had accumulated by their oppressive measures, and pointed out to him how easily this wealth might be used to subvert his authority. It would be charitable to suppose that the Khan, when he consented to the extreme measure of depriving them of life, acted on the firm conviction that his suspicions of their treasonable designs were well-founded; it does not, however, appear that he had strong grounds for his suspicions, and he seems rather to have yielded to the advice of interested persons. That he should have found it necessary, in deposing his ministers, to imbrue his hands in their blood, shows either the frail tenure of his authority, or that he was actuated by great hatred of them. Such acts are too common in these despotic countries to excite surprise; but however necessary they may sometimes be to self-preservation, it is difficult to excuse the cool treachery which too frequently accompanies them. In the present instance, the victims, whether of their own imprudence or of the machinations of their enemies, became previously acquainted with the fate which awaited them. They were aware of the measures secretly taken to watch their movements and prevent all chance of escape, while outwardly no change occurred in the Khan's behaviour towards them. They continued their daily attendance at his court, and were received with increased kindness and attention. They transacted his affairs as usual; and though in hourly expectation of the impending blow, they dared not betray their suspicions, for fear of hastening their fate and depriving themselves of the still small hope they entertained of the Khan's relenting. On the day appointed for their execution, the Khan held his court in his palace at Ahmedpur, to which they were summoned. After dismissing the Durbar, he withdrew, but requested the ministers to wait for his return, as he had something further which he wished to communicate to them. A few minutes elapsed, when a Kidmutghar was sent to them to request their attendance in another apartment of the palace where the Khan was in the habit of receiving them in private. To reach this apartment, they had to pass through a court-yard; and here they were met and stopped in their progress by Mohammed Yakoob Khas Kheilee and eight or ten armed men. Their swords were snatched from them; and they were told that they were traitors to the Khan, and must die. They protested their innocence, but offered no resistance. The only boon they craved from their murderers, was to be allowed to offer up a prayer to their God and to Mohammed, the prophet of all Mussulmans. This was granted; and they were afterwards quickly despatched. Their murder was followed by the plunder of their house and property; but news of their death had previously reached their wretched relatives; and then the usual sequel to such catastrophes ensued, in the indiscriminate slaughter by a surviving brother of all the female inmates of the family. The brother himself, with a few followers, died in defending the entrance to their common home, which was afterwards pillaged by the Khan's people, led on by Mohammed Daim Khas Kheilee. Two infant sons were spared, although the new minister, Mohammed Yakoob, is said to have wished their death, observing that the young of the serpent become serpents when they grow old. The Khan compassionated their youth, and had them brought up with his own son of the same age, and provided tutors for their instruction.

After the death of Sheikh Mukbool and Sheikh Noor Mohammed, the Khas Kheilee Mohammed Yakoob, Mohammed Kaim and Mohammed Daim, enjoyed an unlimited authority. Mohammed Yakoob was promoted to the office of Vizir, and Mohammed Kaim to the office of Bukshee to the forces.

Bahawal Khan continued to pay Nuzrana to the Lahore chief for the country about Multan, Dereh Ghazi Khan, and the opposite side of the river. The Maharajah increased the Nuzrana every year, until at last it amounted to five lakhs. Whenever he sent a force to levy the tribute, the Khan's people withdrew, leaving the country to be plundered. This continued till 1831, when a force was sent under General Ventura to demand all the arrears of tribute, amounting to seven lakhs. The Khan's officers retreated as they advanced, leaving the country open to them, in the full expectation that, after plundering as much as they could, they would again retire; but Ventura, having obtained the Maharajah's permission to that effect, occupied the country, and strengthened himself as he advanced, posting Thanas and officers at the different towns to regulate the police and to collect the revenue. The Khan made some efforts to renew his engagements with the Maharajah, but without success, owing to mismanagement and the peculations of his officers. The country latterly had hardly brought him in five lakhs of rupees; whereas General Ventura, on first taking charge of it, bound himself to pay eleven lakhs into the Maharajah's treasury for the first year.

APPENDIX.

No. I.

PRESENT STATE OF BAHAWALPUR.

THE territory now remaining to Bahawal Khan on the left bank of the Sutlej and the Indus, extends in length about 230 koss from Rana Wuttoo on the north-east frontier, to within a mile of Subzul-Kot on the south-west. To the north and north-west it is bounded by the river Sutlej and Indus. To the south and south-west, by Jeyselmeer and the territory of the Ameers of Sindh; to the east and north-east, by Bikaner, the Bhuttee country, Kote Kuppoora, and the territory of Mundote, subject to the Lahore chief. Its limits in the desert, extending in a circle from north-east to south and south-west, may be loosely determined by the situation of the forts of Goorjiana or Futteghur, Wulhur, Pholehra, Meerghur, Tihara, Rukimpur, Khanghur, Bijroth, and Islamghur. The tract of cultivated country intervening between the rivers and the desert throughout the whole extent of this territory, varies in breadth from one to eighteen miles.

The present actual revenue of the Bahawalpur state is not supposed to exceed ten lakhs of rupees; of this sum, five lakhs are paid into the Khan's treasury. Territory, producing four lakhs, is disposed of to Jaghirdars on condition of military service; and the remaining lakh consists of grants of land to religious and learned persons bestowed unconditionally.

The amount of revenue paid into the Khan's treasury is realized from the following sources:—

Custom and transit duties on merchandize, 1 lakh of rupees.

Sale of indigo produced in the Khan's territories, 1 lakh.

Ditto of grain of every description, 2½ lakhs.

Ditto of cotton produced in the Khan's territories, 15,000 rupees.

Pasturage and fines levied from pastoral predatory tribes, 35,000 rupees.

The Jaghirdars holding lands on condition of military service to the state, compose the Khan's principal force. They amount to 8,000 men, chiefly Daoodputras. Of these, 2,000 are Shuttur Sawars, 2,000 are Horsemen, and 4,000 are Foot Soldiers.

To each man are allotted fifty Beegahs of land. If the Jaghirdar cultivates his own land, he takes the Zemindar's share, and divides the Sirkar's share on the fifty beegahs between himself and the Sirkar. If he cultivates his lands by Asamees or Ryots, after they have received their share, whatever it may be, the remainder is divided between the Sirkar and Jaghirdar; so that in reality the Jaghirdar only pays revenue for twenty-five Beegahs. These Jaghirdars are termed Jaghirdar Lushkur Kush Kusurdar; the latter name applies to the nature of the tenure by which they hold these lands, cultivating fifty Beegahs and paying revenue for twenty-five Beegahs only. Whenever this force is employed by the Khan on service, each man gets one seer of atta, with a trifle of salt and ghee, for his daily subsistence; but receives no pay.

The other forces maintained by the Khan consist of, 1st. Five regiments of regular infantry; the whole of which together do not muster more than twelve or thirteen hundred men. They are a miserable rabble without a shadow of discipline, and consist chiefly of Purbeeas, run-away Sipahis from the eastward. 2nd. Twelve hundred Bazegur horsemen; the horse and arms are the property of the Sirkar. The men receive two rupees' worth of rations, and six rupees pay per month. They are chiefly kept in attendance on the Khan and his principal officers. 3rd. Five hundred foreign horse or Muzuffir Sawars. The men furnish their own horses and arms, and receive from ten to twelve rupees a month pay. The forts in the desert are garrisoned by foot soldiers, chiefly of the Mahur caste; their number is stated at 2,200 men.

The artillery consists of sixteen guns; for eight of which, the establishment of Goolandas and bullocks is kept up. There are said to be upwards of forty guns, including those in the forts; but few are in a serviceable state.

No. II.

REMARKS ON THE BELOOCH TRIBES, INHABITING THE COUNTRY TO THE WEST OF THE INDUS, DEPENDENT ON DEREH GHAZI KHAN.

THE track of country lying between the Indus and the Suleiman range of mountains, included between the latitudes of Sanghar and Umarkot, and dependent on Dereh Ghazi Khan, is inhabited by Belooch tribes, mixed, as they approach the river, with Jats and other Mussulman Zemindars inferior in number.

Of the Belooch tribes, beginning from the north and proceeding southwards, the principal are as follows:—

1st. The Nutkanis, whose chief place is Sanghar, and the residence of the family of their chief, Tonsa. They muster about 3,000 fighting men. Their country, being irrigated on one side by water from the Indus, and on the other by mountain streams, is rich and fertile; producing in abundance wheat, barley and rice, with sugar-cane, indigo, cotton, mustard, and most of the smaller kinds of grain and pulse common to Upper Hindustan. Buffalos and cows are reared in considerable numbers; but the chief property of those who reside in the hills consists in large flocks of goats and sheep of the Dumba kind. A very valuable breed of camels for burden is also found there. Assad Khan, the chief of this tribe, has continued a state prisoner at Multan ever since the occupation of the territory dependent on Dereh Ghazi Khan by the Sikh troops under General Ventura. He is nearly related to the Nawab of Bahawalpur, between whom and the present governor of Multan, negotiations have been long pending for his release; but this would seem as far off as ever, the price demanded for his ransom being much greater than the Nawab is inclined to give.

2nd. The Khosas, whose chief place is Gujri, and the name of their chief, Kauri Khan. Their country is poor and badly watered, producing little grain; but the hilly parts of it abound in sheep and cattle. The tribe are pastoral in their habits, but unsettled, and robbers by profession; and formerly paid little revenue save what was extorted from them by dint of force.

3rd. The Lagharis, whose chief places of abode are, Khota in the plains and Barkhan in the hills. Their country is barren, depending chiefly for water on the rains, which are very precarious. The head of their tribe is Rahun Khan. They muster upwards of 2,000 fighting men, and furnish Badrikas or guards through their own territories and the territories of the Gurchanis and Bugtis, to Kafilas coming and going from Khelat to Dereh Ghazi Khan and Arsué in the vicinity of Mithan-Kot.

4th. The Lunds, whose chief place is Tibi, near Harrand. The head of their tribe is Mohammed Khan. They muster something less than 1,000 fighting men, and their country is poor and barren.

5th. The Gurchanis, whose chief place is Lalgarh in the hills opposite to Harrand. They muster above 2,000 fighting men, and are extremely predatory in their habits. The name of their chief is Khoti Khan. Their country depends chiefly on the rains for cultivation, and is consequently poor and barren.

6th. The Drishaks, who reside at Fatehpur, Kotla, and Arsué. This tribe is divided into three branches under different leaders. They make use of wells for cultivation as well as of the water of the river; and their country is productive. They are also rich in cattle. Their number is from 1,500 to 2,000.

REMARKS.

1st. During the Afghan monarchy, these tribes held Jaghirs from the Hakims of Dereh Ghazi Khan on condition of rendering military service for the protection of the dependencies of that place from the predatory inroads of the Beloochees of the Berohee country more to the westward. They also paid revenue in kind to the Hakims of Dereh Ghazi Khan in the proportion of one-fourth or one-fifth of the whole produce; but this was seldom realised to the whole amount. Their general character was predatory. They engaged little in cultivation, depending for support chiefly on their flocks and herds, and on the plunder of the neighbouring districts on either side of the Indus. That portion of their country which is irrigated by the waters of the Indus is rich, while the hills which they inhabit, comprising the first low range of the Suleiman Mountains, are barren and rocky, and for the most part destitute of water. Grass and a few stunted trees of the

Karinjal and Lai, with the Lasura (a species of camel grass), including mines, from which is extracted an inferior kind of alum, comprehend all their natural productions. Scanty crops of wheat, and of the smaller kinds of grain, are sometimes raised after a fall of rain in the cold weather, and after a favourable monsoon. On these occasions, the plains skirting the hills are abandoned by the Beloochees, who retire into hills, where they remain till their supply of water is exhausted. Owing, however, to the paucity of rain which falls in these countries, these temporary absences from the plains can occur but seldom. When pressed by the Hakims for arrears of revenue, or called on to restore plundered property, it was also a custom with them to retire into the hills, where they were often suffered to remain unmolested until obliged by their own wants to descend again into the plains. Owing to the constant change of Hakims at Dereh Ghazi Khan, they not unfrequently by these means escaped with impunity, after being guilty of the most flagrant acts of rebellion and plunder, but when, as sometimes happened, they had to deal with a resolute governor determined on punishing them for their misdeeds, the movement of a small body of troops into their hills, where they had no strongholds or means of defence beyond the barren and difficult nature of the country, obliged them at once either to come in and sue for pardon, or to throw themselves for protection and assistance into the hands of the Belooch tribes of the Berohee country. They usually preferred trusting to the clemency of the governor to having recourse to these neighbours, between whom and themselves strong feuds always existed: but in case they pursued the latter course, their appeal for assistance was never made in vain; and the consequence was, a sudden inroad of 5,000 or 6,000 men into the plains, which, from the Hakims being unprepared to resist so large a force, were generally laid waste, the villages plundered and destroyed, and the cattle and other moveable property carried off by the plunderers.

"Of the Belooch tribes of the Berohee country, beginning from the north and proceeding in a south-west direction, the following are the principal:—The Buzdars, the Marries, the Berohees, the Bugtees, the Dumkees, and Kharpals. Each of these tribes musters from 4,000 to 6,000 fighting men. They are nominally only subject to the Berohee chief; and their plundering propensities, from his total inability to coerce them, have of late years entirely put a stop to the trade once carried on between Multan, Khelat, and Candahar. To the south of them, inhabiting the plains in the neighbourhood of Umarkot, are the Mazarees, a Belooch tribe, nominally subject to the Ameers of Sindh. Their chief place, and the residence of their chief, Bahram Khan, is Rujhan. They number about four thousand fighting men, They are more predatory in their habits than any of the tribes hitherto mentioned, and carry their depredations alike into the Sindh, Lahore, and Bahawalpur territories."

It was only by leaguing themselves with these freebooters, and by their sudden predatory inroads, as above described, that the Beloochees of the plains and hills, subject to Dereh Ghazi Khan, could ever render themselves in any way formidable to the ruling power. Their desperate internal feuds, not less than the extreme poverty of their chiefs, prevented all chance of extensive combination among them; and in this respect the Belooch tribes to the westward did not differ from them. When assembled at the call of their chief, it was the custom for each man of a tribe to take with him provisions for four or five days, and as soon as these were exhausted he returned to his home. The chiefs, unable themselves to provide them with necessaries, had no authority over them to prevent their dispersing. Their avarice, which is not less proverbial than their poverty, and their habitual treachery towards each other, made the task of controlling them comparatively easy.

In their predatory incursions, the Beloochees are said to make astonishingly long journeys both on foot and on horseback. Those of the hills and many of those of the plains are mounted on small ponies of a hardy breed, accustomed to the rough and stony roads they have to travel over. They all dismount to fight: their chief weapons are the sword and buckler; and their usual mode of attack is to form a line of single ranks, and tying themselves together round the waist by their long waistbands, to move in that order towards their adversaries, commencing with a deliberate step, which is increased to full speed as they mutually approach. They also use the matchlock, but discard it after the first fire, or carry it in the left hand across the shield. They are but little accustomed to fire-arms of any description. Though known to fight desperately against each other in their party feuds, the mere sound of a cannon has been found sufficient to scare thousands of them from the field.

After the decline of the Afghan monarchy, the territory dependent on Dereh Ghazi Khan was taken possession of by Maharajah Runjeet Sing; but it is necessary here to remark, that many portions of it, such as the districts of Dhaka Silpur, Mithan-Kot, and Nashaira, were farmed from the Hakims of Dereh Ghazi Khan, on the part of the Afghan kings, by the Daoodputras of Garih, a branch of the Bahawalpur family, long before they came into the possession of the Lahore government. In 1819 A. D., when Dereh Ghazi Khan itself was wrested from the hands of its governor, Goman Khan (Jubbar Khan ?) by Maharajah Runjeet Sing, it was then made over in farm with the whole of the territory dependent on it, to the Nawab of Bahawalpur, Sadik Mohammed Khan, under whom and his successor, the present Nawab, it remained till 1831, when the troops and officers of the latter were driven across the river, and the country occupied by the Lahore troops under General Ventura.

The Belooch tribes were well affected towards the Bahawalpur government; and while under its rule, the country near the Indus suffered comparatively little from their excesses. This was owing more to the knowledge of their character possessed by the Bahawalpur officers, than to the strength of the government itself. By artfully fomenting their internal differences, they left them less leisure to prey upon their more peaceable and industrious neighbours; but it will be readily conceived, that while in this disturbed state, little revenue was realised from the Beloochees themselves; none whatever reached the government, while its subordinate officers enriched themselves by taking a fourth share of all plunder, a tax willingly paid by the Zemindars for the liberty allowed them of indulging in a mode of life every way congenial to their habits. On one occasion, to punish an inroad of the Berohee Beloochees, Nawab Sadik Mohammed Khan sent a force of two hundred horsemen and some infantry into the hills, and established an outpost at Barkhan, where there was a small Gurhee; finding, however, the expence of supporting the detachment there not balanced by the benefits derived from it, it was withdrawn, after having been kept there upwards of a year.

Native reports mention that at the distance of a short day's journey from Barkhan, is a Darra or mountain-pass, conducting by a direct road through Ghazni to Cabul, the entrance to which has been closed for a number of years, and apparently with great labour, by rolling stones and rocks into it for the distance of half a mile; that this Darra was formerly frequented by Kafilas; and that the whole route from Dereh Ghazi Khan through it to Cabul, is practicable for artillery, and was formerly frequented by Kafilas; and a road is said to branch off from it and conduct straight to Candahar.

2nd.—On General Ventura taking possession of Dereh Ghazi Khan, the chiefs of the Belooch tribes, before described as holding Jaghirs dependent on that place, came in at his invitation, and on acknowledging submission to the Lahore government, were confirmed in their possessions. By a well-directed liberality and conciliatory measures, he made himself extremely popular among them; and the large force which he kept up, while it effectually checked the incursions of the more westerly tribes, enabled him also to put a stop to the internal commotions prevailing among the tribes in the Dereh Ghazi Khan territory, and to realise a revenue from them with little difficulty.

On Dewan Sawan Mall's succeeding to the government of Dereh Ghazi Khan, in compliance with the wishes of Maharajah Runjeet Sing, he obliged the Belooch chiefs and Zemindars to enter into engagements to pay their revenue in money instead of in kind. This measure, which was received by them as a direct innovation on their rights, created great dissatisfaction at the time; and though a fifth of the government share of revenue was afterwards remitted in consequence, they never became reconciled to it, and frequently appealed against it, but in vain. In other respects, the Dewan's rule was mild; and, owing to the strict regard he paid to his engagements, and the rigid superintendance he exercised over all the revenue officers under him, could not but have been popular. Notwithstanding the difficulties he had to contend with in the outset, he succeeded in preserving internal tranquillity among his Belooch subjects without suffering them to fall into arrears in the payment of their revenue. He was not, however, so fortunate in preserving his frontier from the inroads of the Beloochees more to the westward. On General Ventura's recall to Lahore, a large proportion of the force stationed by him on this frontier was withdrawn also; but, what was a greater loss, the moral check of his name, which had hitherto contributed so much to restrain these rude and ignorant people, was no longer present. Added to this, Dewan Sawan Mall, though a most active and able officer, owing to the immense extent of territory which he had under his charge, was frequently obliged to be absent, settling affairs at one extremity, when his presence was most required at the other. These causes combining, emboldened the Beloochees, and especially the Mazaree tribe, to shake off what had been felt by them as an intolerable restraint, and to return to their predatory habits; and although the Dewan took measures to check them, by ordering forts to be constructed at Dajal Harrand and Umarkot, he could not altogether prevent his subjects suffering from their aggressions. On two occasions, he assembled a force and marched into the territory of the Mazarees; and, but for the known objections of the Lahore chief, would have established a Thana at the chief town, Rujhun. On the last of these occasions, in the cold weather of 1833-34, Bahram Khan, the chief of the Mazarees, came in himself to the Dewan, who not only made him restore the cattle stolen from his Mithankot subjects, but exacted from him, under the name of a Nuzrana to the Lahore chief, the payment of a sum of money, besides a number of camels, horses, and cattle; and, at the same time, made him enter into engagements, under a heavy penalty, to refrain from all future aggressions. How these engagements have been observed will be seen from the short account of recent occurrences on the Sindh frontier, extracted from the news-writer's reports, which accompany this paper.

Ahmedpur, (Signed) F. MACKISON,
14th May, 1835. British Agent.

No. III.

TREATY CONCLUDED BETWEEN THE HONOURABLE EAST INDIA COMPANY AND NAWAB BAHAWAL KHAN, THE RULER OF BAHAWALPUR, DATED THE 2ND FEBRUARY, 1833.

By the blessing of God, the friendly connection between the Honourable the East India Company and the state of Bahawalpur, which commenced on the occasion of the Hon. Mr. Elphinstone's visit to Cabul in 1808-9, has continued uninterrupted to the present time; and now that Captain C. M. Wade, political agent at Loodianah, has arrived at Bahawalpur on the part of the Right Hon. Lord W. Bentinck, G.C.B., G.C.H., the Governor-General of British India, in order to improve these amicable relations, and concert the opening of the navigation of the rivers Indus and Sutlej, with a view to promote the general interest of commerce, which is pleasing to God, and the prosperity of the surrounding states, the following are the articles of a treaty which has been concluded through the agency of that officer between the Honourable the East India Company on the one part, and Nawab Kuken-ud-Dowla Hafizul-Mulk Mukhlis-ud-Dowla Mohammed Bahawal Khan Abbasee, Nusret Jung Behauder, the chief of the Daoodputras, on the other, for the purpose of confirming the friendship of the two states, the opening of the trade by the above-mentioned rivers, and regulating the manner in which the arrangements connected with it are to be carried into effect.

Article I.—There shall be eternal friendship and alliance between the Honourable the East India Company and Nawab Mohammed Bhaul Kahawl, his heirs and successors.

Art. II.—The Honourable the East India Company engage never to interfere with the hereditary or other possessions of the Bahawalpur government.

Art. III.—As regards the internal administration of his government, and the exercise of his sovereign right over his subjects, the Nawab shall be entirely independent as heretofore.

Art. IV.—The officer who may be appointed on the part of the British Government to reside in the Bahawalpur state, shall, in conformity with the preceding article, abstain from all interference with the Nawab's government, and shall respect the preservation of the friendly relations of the two contracting parties.

Art. V.—The Honourable the East India Company having requested the use of the rivers Indus and Sutlej, and the roads of Bahawalpur for the merchants of Hindustan, etc., the government of Bahawalpur agrees to grant the same through its own boundaries, if the persons aforesaid be provided with passports.

Art. VI.—The government of Bahawalpur engages to fix, in concert with the British Government, certain proper and moderate duties, to be levied on merchandise proceeding by the aforesaid route, and never to increase or diminish the same without the consent of both parties.

Art. VII.—It is further agreed, that the tariff, or table of duties fixed as above, shall be published for general information; and the custom-house officers and farmers of the revenues of the Bahawalpur government will be especially directed not to detain the passing trade, after having collected the duties, on pretence of waiting for fresh orders from their government, or any other pretext.

Art. VIII.—The tariff which is to be established for the line of navigation in question, is intended to apply exclusively to the passage of merchandise by that route, and not to interfere with the transit duties levied on goods proceeding from one bank of the river to the other, or with the established Choku inland; these will remain as heretofore.

Art. IX.—Merchants frequenting the said route, while within the limits of the Nawab's government, are required to show a due regard to his authority, as is done by merchants generally, and not to commit any act offensive to the civil and religious institutions of the country.

Art. X.—The proportion of duties to which the Nawab may be entitled, shall be collected by his officers at the appointed places.

Art. XI.—The officers who are to be entrusted with the examination of the goods and collection of the duties on the part of the Bahawalpur government, shall be stationed opposite to Methankote and Hurreeke; at no other place but those two shall boats in transit on the river be liable to examination or stoppage.

Art. XII.—When the persons in charge of boats stop of their own accord, to take in or give out cargo, the goods will be liable to the local transit duty of the Bahawalpur government, previously to their being embarked, and subsequently to their being landed, as provided in Article VIII.

Art. XIII.—The superintendant stationed opposite to Mithenkote having examined the cargo, will levy the established duty and grant a passport, with a written account of the cargo and freight. On the arrival of the boat at Hurreeke, the superintendant at that station will compare the passport with the cargo, and whatever goods are found in excess, will be liable to the payment of the established duty, while the rest, having already paid duty at Mithenkote, will pass on free.

Art. XIV.—The same regulation shall be in force for merchandise coming from Hurreeke towards Sindh.

....

Art. XV.—With regard to the safety of merchants who may frequent this route, the Nawab's officers will afford them every protection in their power; and whenever merchants may happen to halt for the night, it will be incumbent on them to show their passport to the Thanadar, or other officer in authority at the place, and demand their protection.

Art. XVI.—The articles of the present treaty shall in all respects, whether relating to the internal government of the Nawab's country, or to commerce, be mutually observed, and form an everlasting bond of friendship between the two states.

Dated at Bahawalpur, the 22d February, 1833.

(Signed) H. C. Bentinck.

Ratified by the Governor-General in Council, on the 13th September, 1833.

No. IV.

ARTICLES OF A SUPPLEMENTARY TREATY BETWEEN THE HONOURABLE EAST INDIA COMPANY, AND THE GOVERNMENT OF BAHAWALPUR.

Whereas in the sixth article of the treaty concluded between the Honourable the East India Company and the Bahawalpur Government, dated 22d February, 1833, it was stipulated, that a moderate scale of duties should be fixed by the two Governments in concert, to be levied on all merchandise in transit up and down the rivers Indus and Sutlej, the said Governments being now of opinion, that owing to the inexperience of these countries in such matters, the mode of levying duties then proposed (viz on the value and quantity of goods) could not fail to give rise to mutual misunderstandings and reclamations, have, with a view to prevent these results, determined to substitute a toll, which shall be levied on all boats with whatever merchandise laden. The following articles have therefore been adopted as supplementary to the former treaty; and in conformity with them, each Government engages that the toll shall be levied, and its amount neither be increased nor diminished, except with the consent of both parties.

Art. I.—A toll of 570 rupees shall be levied on all boats laden with merchandise, in transit on the rivers Indus and Sutlej, between the sea and Roopur, without reference to their size, or to the weight or value of their cargo, the above toll to be divided among the different states, in proportion to the extent of territory which they possess on the banks of these rivers.

Art. II.—The portion of the above toll appertaining to the Bahawalpur state, and amounting to rupees 106 2¼, shall be levied opposite to Mithenkote, on boats coming from the sea towards Roopur, and in the vicinity of Hurreeke Petten, on boats going from Roopur towards the sea, and at no other place.

Art. III.—In order to facilitate the realisation of the toll due to the different states, as well as for the speedy and satisfactory adjustment of any dispute which may arise connected with the safety of the navigation, and the welfare of the trade by the new route, a British officer will reside near Mithenkote, and a native agent on the part of the British Government in the vicinity of the Hurreeke Petten. These officers will be subject to the orders of the British agent at Loodianah; and the agents who may be appointed to reside at those places on the part of the other states concerned in the navigation, will co-operate with them in the execution of their duties.

Art. IV.—The British Government binds itself, that the British officer who may reside near Mithenkote, shall not engage in trade; and (in conformity with the fourth article of the former treaty) that he shall not interfere in any way with the internal administration of the Bahawalpur Government.

Art. V.—In order to guard against imposition on the part of merchants in making false complaints of being plundered of property which they never possessed, they are required, when taking out their passports, to produce an invoice of their cargo, which being duly authenticated, a copy of it will be annexed to their passport.

Art. VI.—Such parts of the 6th, 7th, 11th, 13th, and 14th articles of the treaty of the 22d February, 1833, as have reference to the fixing of a duty on the value and quantity of merchandise, and to the mode of its collection, are hereby rescinded, and the foregoing articles substituted in their place, agreeably to which, and the conditions of the preamble, the toll shall be levied.

(True copy and translation.) (Signed) C. M. Wade,
Political Agent, &c.
(Signed) W. C. Bentinck.

Ratified by the Governor-General in Council on the 5th March, 1835.

No. V.

DETAILED STATEMENT OF THE AMOUNT OF TOLLS LEVIABLE IN THE BAHAWALPUR TERRITORY, ON BOATS PROCEEDING UP AND DOWN THE RIVERS INDUS AND SUTLEJ.

Whereas by the treaty of the 27th of the month of Shahban, 1250 Hijra, agreeing with the 29th of the month of December, 1834 A.D., the Bahawalpur Government is entitled, on account of the whole extent of its territory, to levy, at the appointed places, a toll of 106 rupees, 12 annas, and 3 pie on all boats laden with merchandise proceeding from Roopur towards the sea, or from the sea towards Roopur, the same will continue in force; but as some of the boats are found not to pass through the whole extent of the Bahawalpur territory, but, on the contrary, to lay in cargoes at, and set out from, or dispose of their cargoes at, and return from, places on the way, it is therefore agreed, that on such boats the amount of toll to be levied shall be regulated by the relative distances of the places from which, after laying in a cargo, they take their departure, or from which, after disposing of their goods, they return, as follows:—

1st. On all boats laden with merchandise proceeding from beyond the eastern frontier of the Bahawalpur territory, to Kheirpur Shangia, and *vice versâ*, the Bahawalpur Government is entitled to levy, both in coming and going, on account of river toll, the sum noted in the margin . . Rs 53 6 1½

Ditto, ditto, from beyond the frontier to Bahawalpur, and *vice versâ* . . . . „ 66 11 8

Ditto, ditto, from beyond the eastern frontier to Chachram, and *vice versâ* . . . . . . „ 93 6 8½

Ditto, ditto, from beyond the north eastern frontier to the S. W. frontier, and *vice versâ* „ 106 12 3

2d. In the same manner on all boats laden with merchandise proceeding from beyond the south-eastern frontier to Chachram, and *vice versâ*, the Bahawalpur Government is entitled to levy, both in coming and going, on account of river toll, the sum noted in the margin . . . . Rs. 13 5 6

Ditto, ditto, from beyond the S. W. frontier to Bahawalpur, and *vice versâ* . . . . . . „ 40 0 6

On all boats, from beyond the S. W. frontier to Kheirpur, and *vice versâ*. . . . . . . „ 53 6 1½

On all boats, from beyond the S. W. frontier
to the N. E. frontier, and *vice versâ* . . Rs. 106 12 3

3d. On all boats laden with merchandise from the rivers of the Punjab, that enter the channel of the Sutlej and Indus, opposite the ferry of Bakri, if they proceed from the above ferry to beyond the S. W. frontier to Bahawalpur territory, and into foreign territory, or *vice versâ*, the Bahawalpur Government is entitled to levy, on account of river toll, and according to the extent of his territory traversing, the sum noted in the margin . . . . Rs. 26 11 0¾

Ditto, ditto, on boats proceeding from the ferry of Bakri, to beyond the N. E. frontier, and into foreign territory, and *vice versâ* . . „ 80 1 2½

4th. On empty boats no duty is to be levied.

5th. At whatever place in the Bahawalpur territory merchants may stop to lay in, or dispose of cargo, agreeably to the former territories, they will pay the established duties of that place on the purchase and sale of goods.

(Signed) F. Mackison.

Approved by the Governor-General of India, on the 11th October, 1833.

No. VI.

PROPOSED RATES FOR THE NAVIGATION OF THE SUTLEJ AND THE INDUS BY MERCANTILE BOATS (EXCEPTING THE NAWAB BAHAWAL KHAN'S OWN MERCHANTS AND SUBJECTS), TO BE PAID FOR THE TRANSIT THROUGH THE BAHAWALPUR TERRITORY.

Art. I.—Grain, wood, and limestone, free as in the Lahore territory.

Art. II.—Besides the above three things, duties to be levied on all sorts of merchandise, according to three sizes of boats.

Art. III.—A boat not capable of containing more than 250 maunds of freight, proceeding from Rojhan, or Kote Mithem, to the front of the hills, Roopur, Loodiana, etc.; from Roopur or Loodiana, to Rojhan, or Kote Mithem Rs. 10 0 0

A boat above 250 Maunds and not exceeding 500 Mds. . . . . „ 20 0 0

A boat above 500 Maunds . . . . „ 40 0 0

Art. IV.—No. 1, 2, 3, to be written in large letters on all boats, to show the class to which each boat belongs.

Dated 5th August, 1840, corresponding with 5th Jummad-oos-sanne, 1256, Hijra.

(True Translation.)

(Signed) George Clerk,
Adjt. Gov. General.

Sanctioned by the Governor-General of India, in council, on the 31st August, 1840.

No. VII.

AGREEMENT REGARDING THE LEVY OF DUTIES IN MERCHANDISE IN TRANSIT, THROUGH THE BAHAWALPUR STATE (EXCEPTING THE MERCHANTS AND MERCANTILE FIRMS, THE PROPER SUBJECTS OF THE BAHAWALPUR STATE), THE FOLLOWING ARTICLES HAVE BEEN AGREED TO BETWEEN THE BRITISH AND BAHAWALPUR GOVERNMENTS.

First.—On boats freighted with merchandise going up or down the river, through the Bahawalpur country, the duties shall be only one-half of the present fixed rates.

Second.—On merchandise passing in any direction by land, no other duties shall be levied than the following, viz:—

On a hackery laden with merchandise . . .	Rs.	2	0	0
On a camel ditto, ditto	„	1	0	0
On a mule, pony, bullock, or an ass, ditto, ditto	„	0	8	0

Third.—Any merchant having with him a passport, or "rowanah," according to the form annexed to this agreement, shall pass safe, unmolested, and without search by the local officer on the road.

Fourth.—If any merchant buy or sell the merchandise at any place or town on the road, he will have to pay there the usual local duties.

Fifth.—As there exist no pukhee wells and caravanseries, for the use of travellers on the road from Bahawalpur to Sirsae, the Bahawalpur Government will, throughout its jurisdiction, at every stage, prepare pukhee wells and caravanseries for the comfort of travellers, as well as a road along that route, and keep it in order by taking constant care to keep it in repair.

Sixth.—This agreement has been drawn up in accordance with the friendship subsisting between the two governments, and in order that merchants may satisfactorily, and in full confidence, be engaged in the trade.

Dated 15th Shaban, 1259 Hijra, corresponding with 11th September, 1843, Anno Domini.

(True Translation.)

(Signed) R. N. C. Hamilton.

Notified in the "Calcutta Gazette," by order of the Governor-General of India in council, on the 28th October, 1843.

No. VIII.

TREATY BETWEEN THE ENGLISH EAST INDIA COMPANY AND NAWAB BAHAWAL KHAN BAHADUR, THE NAWAB OF BAHAWALPUR, CONCLUDED BY LIEUTENANT MACKISON, ON THE PART OF THE HONOURABLE COMPANY, IN VIRTUE OF FULL POWERS GRANTED BY THE RIGHT HONOURABLE GEORGE LORD AUCKLAND, G.C.B., GOVERNOR GENERAL OF INDIA, AND BY MOONSHI CHOWKAS RAI, ON THE PART OF THE NAWAB BAHAWAL KHAN BAHADUR, ACCORDING TO FULL POWERS GIVEN BY THE NAWAB.

ARTICLE I.—There shall be perpetual friendship, alliance, and unity of interests between the Honourable Company and Nawab Bahawal Khan Bahadur, and his heirs and successors; and the friends and enemies of one party shall be the friends and enemies of both parties.

Art. II.—The British Government engages to protect the principality and territory of Bahawalpur.

Art. III.—Nawab Bahawal Khan, and his heirs and successors, will act in subordinate co-operation with the British Government, and acknowledge its supremacy, and will not have any connections with any other chiefs or states.

Art. IV.—The Nawab, and his heirs and successors, will not enter into negotiation with any chief or state, without the knowledge and sanction of the British Government, but the usual amicable correspondences with friends and relations shall continue.

Art. V.—The Nawab, and his heirs and successors, will not commit aggressions on any one. If by accident any dispute arise with any one, the settlement of it shall be submitted to the arbitration and award of the British Government.

Art. VI.—The Nawab of Bahawalpur will furnish troops at the requisition of the British Government, according to his means.

Art. VII.—The Nawab, and his heirs and successors, shall be absolute rulers of their country, and the British jurisdiction shall not be introduced into that principality.

Art. VIII.—This treaty of seven articles having been concluded, and signed and sealed by Lieutenant Mackison and Moonshi Chowkas Rai; the ratifications by the Right Honourable the Governor-General and Bahawal Khan Bahadur, shall be exchanged within forty days from the present date.

Done at Ahmedpur, this 5th day of October, A.D. 1838, corresponding with the 14th of Rajabul Murajub, 1254, Hijra.

(Signed) AUCKLAND.

Ratified and confirmed by the Right Honourable the Governor-General, at Simla, the 22nd of October, Anno Domini, 1838.

THE END.

PEDIGREE OF THE BAHAWALPUR FAMILY.

Bahawal Khan - - - - - -	III.
Sadik Khan - - - - - - -	II.
Bahawal Khan - - - - - -	II.
Fatteh Khan - - - - - - -	
Bahawal Khan - - - - - -	I.
Mobarik Khan - - - - - - -	II.
Sadik Mohammed Khan - - - - -	I.
Mobarik Khan - - - - - - -	I.
Bahader Khan - - - - - - -	II.
Feeroz Khan - - - - - - -	
Mohammed Khan - - - - - -	II.
Bhaker Khan - - - - - - -	II.
Bahader Khan - - - - - - -	I.
Bhaker Khan - - - - - - -	I.
Heibut Khan - - - - - - -	
Fatteh Khan - - - - - - -	
Chander Khan - - - - - - -	
Daood Khan - - - - - - -	II.
Mohammed Khan - - - - - -	I.
Mahmood Khan - - - - - -	I.
Daood Khan - - - - - - -	
Pehla Khan - - - - - - -	
Chundee Khan Jam - - - - - -	
Johul Khan - - - - - - -	
Singrasee Khan - - - - - -	
Kahar Khan - - - - - - -	
Abbun Khan - - - - - - -	
Sultan Ahmed - - - - - - -	II.
Sultan Shah Maizinal-Akeil - - - -	
Soheil Khan - - - - - - -	

Yaseen - - - - - - - -	
Ahmed - - - - - - - -	1st Calif.
Mohammed - - - - - - -	Do.
Abul-Fozul - - - - - - -	Do.
Aboo-jafir-Abdullah - - - - -	Do.
Mohammed Ameen - - - - - -	Do.
Haroon Rasheed - - - - - -	Do.
Mehdee - - - - - - - -	Do.
Aboojafir - - - - - - -	
Mohammed - - - - - - -	
Ali - - - - - - - -	
Abdullah - - - - - - - -	
Abbas (the Uncle of the Prophet) - - -	

43 men.